THE BECOMING OF G-D

What the Trinitarian nature of God has to do with Church and a deep Spirituality for the Twenty First Century

Ian Mobsby

THE BECOMING OF G-D

What the Trinitarian nature of God has to do with Church and a deep Spirituality for the Twenty First Century

YTC Press
www.ytcpress.com
Monograph Series

YTC Press

An imprint dedicated to research on Youth, Theology & Culture

First published in 2008 by
YTC Press
– A Division of Youth Focus –
www.ytcpress.com
www.youthfocus.biz

ISBN: 978-1-4092-0078-9

Copyright © 2008 Ian Mobsby

All rights reserved. No part of this book may be reproduced or transmitted in any form or by any means, electronic or mechanical, including photocopying, recording, or by any information storage and retrieval system, without permission in writing from the publisher.

Youth Focus

Youth Focus is a partnership dedicated to providing good quality resources for those involved in Christian youth ministry at an affordable price. We undertake this ministry by

- Training volunteer, part-time and full-time youth workers throughout the world through our accredited online Emerge Academy, www.emergeacademy.net
- Providing lecture resources (scripts, handouts and PowerPoint presentations) for those involved in teaching youth ministry and associated disciplines, www.youthfocus.biz
- Publishing books, with our YTC Imprint through www.lulu.com, on youth ministry, ecclesiology, cultural studies, theology, education and associated disciplines

Youth Focus is based in the UK but partners with organisations around the world.

For more information, please contact Steve Griffiths through steve@youthfocus.biz or go to the websites:

www.youthfocus.biz
www.emergeacademy.net
www.ytcpress.com

In grateful memory of Gladys Mary Plant and Sarah Plant.
You were both greatly loved and now greatly missed.

Contents

Preface – page xi

Introduction – page 13

Chapter One – page 15
Experiencing God as Three-yet-One

Chapter Two – page 37
Divine (Open) Ended-ness and Transcendence

Chapter Three – page 51
Ground of Our Being & Our Becoming through God

Chapter Four – page 65
Models and Lessons from the Emerging Church

Chapter Five – page 83
Ancient:Future Church in the 21st Century of the hyper-real

Chapter Six – page 97
Orthopraxis & Sacramentality reframed for the 21st Century

Chapter Seven – page 113
The challenge of human community in a culture of individualism

Chapter Eight – page 133
Trinitarian Devotions

Preface

In 2006 I had the privilege of publishing my MA Dissertation, 'Emerging & Fresh Expressions of Church' through Moot Community Publishing. In that study, which was essentially an investigation into the theology of the emerging Church, I had for the first time come across the incredible depth of Trinitarian informed ecclesiology. The research phase of the study, from 2002 to 2005, was a delightful time of discovery of the deep connection between the Trinity and contemporary experimental expressions of church in a postmodern context. My continued involvement in the Moot Community in London, and the various lectures and talks I have given since have provided me ample opportunity to experience and explore Trinitarianism more fully.

This book is therefore an attempt to reflect on the spiritual implications of the Trinity and in particular the theology of the Cappadocian Fathers who were so influential in helping to conceptualise it. The writing process has been a profound journey of discipleship and self-discovery. For the first time I have had the opportunity to explore the implications of concepts such as perichoresis, kenosis, panentheism and theosis, all of which inter-relate and have profound implications for the church in the twenty first century. I was greatly challenged by the work of Colin Gunton on the Trinity, and in particular, his book "Becoming and Being". This book is named in honour of Gunton's work.

My constant preoccupation with the implications of the Triune God has at times driven my friends completely mad, of this I am sure. The Holy Trinity has been a key motif on my journey with God for at least the last five years. So I want to give thanks to all my friends for their tolerance and support during this project, particularly in the last year.

My grateful thanks go to Aaron Kennedy, editor and critic, who will always be a much better detail person than I will ever be; and to Gareth Powell for formatting the book, and designing the graphics. Thanks also to Mike Radcliffe for the contribution of his ikon and poetry in the devotional chapter of this book, and to all those acknowledged in the devotional chapter concerning the Holy Trinity and Prayer. Finally thanks to Dr Steve Griffiths and YTC Press for being willing to support the creation of this book, and the finally editing process.

It is my hope that this book can in some small way point to the depth of spirituality in Trinitarian theology, aiding and encouraging postmodern pilgrims to dig deep within the Christian tradition to find sustenance and meaning for the journey.

Introduction

Trinitarian theology simply winds some people up, and for many good reasons. For centuries it has been used to promote male dominated, hierarchical and controlling approaches to church structures and the Christian faith. In this form 'Trinitarianism' has been used to exclude, persecute, kill and prevent inter-faith understanding in favour of church power dominance. However, this is not the full tale. The late twentieth century has seen such movements as liberation theology reframe the concept of 'God's-oneness-in-community' to instigate a mission focused on justice and social inclusion. I believe God continues to speak through this paradoxical concept, and that it will prove particularly pertinent for those seeking to re-imagine what it means to be church, and Christian, in the twenty first Century. Our main challenge will be to still our hearts, and attune our ears to the quiet voice with which the Spirit speaks. We must attend to the voice of God amidst the cacophony of competing voices at large in our culture, in an effort to nurture spiritual communities that can then become profound places of God. The odds are perhaps stacked against us, but the rewards of distinctly Christian, contextual expressions of worship, mission and community, will be rich.

So why is this important? Now more than ever we see a Western culture that seeks relationship and belonging but fears it in equal measure. Our post-reformation, post-enlightenment inheritance has been the cult of the individual, and in short, we desire community but often have no idea how to seek it. As a result, our culture has become less humane. The churches have not escaped the scourge of rampant individualism. On one hand some operate like depersonalised corporate businesses, emphasising the 'business' of conversion; and on the other, there are churches that operate like imperialistic establishments, where a certain façade of self-sufficiency is kept in place at all times. Both forms of individualism gravely impoverish the quality of our spiritual communities. Trinitarian theology, I would suggest, is a key to recovering a depth of relationship we have been missing for so long.

It has been said that we live in 'postmodern' times. Whatever the full import of this term, it is clear that personally, spiritually and religiously, these are complex times. Religion it seems has fallen on hard times, while 'spirituality' has emerged as its less institutional, more eclectic successor. The last century has also seen the rise of various fundamentalisms – an approach to life that seeks to simplify complexity by means of rigid edifices of rational, logical thought-systems. Unfortunately these are often deeply dehumanising and devaluing of real community and the relational. Moreover, violence and oppression often go hand in hand with fundamentalism, in and outside of the Church.

It is into this mix that the vibrancy of the Trinity speaks to us, drawing us into intentional forms of relationship that challenge, and change us, to the core of our being. Who is it that we seek when we seek the Lord our God? How does this three-in-one God transform our way of life? How do we live in a strange land where we need to learn social skills, tolerance, and love? What will inspire us to shift from being semi-skilled spiritual tourists, to committed and passionate co-journeying Christian pilgrims? It is the author's contention, and the substance of this book, that God is seeking to draw us into deeper forms of spiritual community and relationality through God's own, experientially revealed nature. The challenge to the church then is whether it is willing to attend to the still, small voice of the God who, like it or not, never stands still.

Chapter One

Experiencing God as Three-yet-One

On a recent trip to a synagogue in central London with members of the Moot community, I was reminded that the Christian God is not that far away from the Jewish one, and that the Christian formulation of the Trinity emerged out of the experience of a long faith tradition, one that is shared between Christians, Jews and Muslims. As I looked through the authorised, revised Jewish prayer book with which the service was conducted, I was very moved by a note at the bottom of one of its pages that stated the following.

'God, the One God has the attributes of Creator, Redeemer and Sustainer.'

These attributes are the very same three words used in many Moot Services[1] to express the paradoxically triune nature of the Christian God. The language is inclusive, and an apt gender-neutral alternative to 'Father, Son and Holy Spirit'. What is common to each of

---

[1] The Moot Community is the Anglican Emerging & Fresh Expression of Church project I am the Priest Missioner to.

the Abrahamic faiths is the understanding that the nature of God emerges out of the varied experience of the Prophets and communities of faith in the Hebrew Scriptures. In this chapter we will explore how the experience of God entered the language of the people of God. We will then draw on the work of a number of writers to explore ways of understanding and speaking of God that avoid the mistakes of the past where God has been conceived of in overly concrete terms.

We will draw on the work of Walter Brueggemann to understand how the language used of God by the Hebrew community evolved out of their experience of God as 'event'. We will then explore briefly the circumstances that eventually gave rise to the doctrine of the Trinity, and how these brought about division in the Church. Finally we will consider how the ancient apophatic tradition, often forgotten in the modern church, offers us a renewed approach to understanding God in postmodern times.

It may seem an obvious thing to say, but belief and faith in God did not emerge out of the minds of clever people; rather, they begin with people having disorientating and transcendent personal experiences of God. The Hebrew and Christian scriptures are a record of the long and varied history of the experiences people have had of God. They are stories, not theological treatises. At the heart of the Trinitarian mystery is the fact that God, previously unknown, chose to actively engage with human beings, and thereby self-reveal something of the divine nature. As we will see later, it took some time for Christians to be able to perceive God as three-in-one. It took the early Church Mothers and Fathers around five hundred years to gather the many hints that pervade Scripture, and articulate the doctrine of the Trinity. Although the essence of the Trinitarian nature of God is present in the scriptural texts, it must be remembered that the word Trinity itself is nowhere to be found. Early church culture was an oral, rather than a word based culture, and therefore many of the creeds were formulated a long time before written texts were commonplace. So as we seek understanding about the Trinitarian nature of God, we must follow the experiential path through which this revelation was received.

Walter Brueggemann, in his exploration of the texts of the Hebrew Scriptures, links language to the self-revelation of God: this is to say that the words and names used of God come directly from the revelatory experience of God.[2] Take for example the word to 'save'.

---

[2] W. Brueggemann, *Theology of the Old Testament*, (Minneapolis: Fortress

Through the experience of having God provide for their needs, the Hebrew people naturally began to describe God as 'the God who saves'. As time went on, through continued positive experience, the relationship was strengthened and the descriptor was expanded so that God was known as 'the God who saves the people'. A further development results in the title, 'the Lord our Saviour'. So with time, people experience the character of God through God's self-revealing activities; the nature of God is experienced, and the language for God develops. It should be noted that the writers of the Hebrew Scriptures were wary of using nouns for God. For example, they are careful when using the term 'Saviour'. Brueggemann gives a convincing argument for why this is so. The use of nouns closes down the meaning and naming of God out of experience, and creates a closed or fixed interpretation. Not using nouns avoided the danger of language defining or controlling the experience of God. Instead, relationship with God is on God's terms, respectful of God's fully volitional, self-determining nature. This closing down and controlling of the language used of God, was the basic form of idolatry. God becomes a fixed abstraction in the minds of human beings, rather than a thinking, choosing, self-revealing, divine being. The main task of the prophets in the Hebrew Scriptures was to prevent this problem by holding nations, their leaders and their priests to account for their idolatrous ways. This old problem persists to this day because it is much easier to live with a controllable approximation of God, rather than an active, changing and totally unpredictable God. The people of God are prone to loosing their way, or becoming controlling, when this kind of idolatry occurs - but much of that later. For now, we have learned that in the ancient world the experience of the self-revealing activity of God is the means by which we learn who God is, what God is like, and therefore how we name God.

Pete Rollins also rightly challenges the objectification of God through language. Fundamentalism, when it claims to know God fully, is unacceptable for the person of faith, for only God fully knows God. Inherent in the acknowledgement that God self-reveals, is the understanding that God also chooses to remain hidden and therefore autonomous over human beings:

> *God's revelation is always surrounded by mystery...The danger of us thinking we know the truth is idolatry. Paul writes*

Press, 1997), 213, 215, 225, 229-30.

> *in Colossians 'see to it that no one takes you captive through hollow and deceptive philosophy, which depends on human tradition and the basic principles of this world rather than on Christ.' [In Colossians 2.8] Paul warns us to beware of human abstractions that draw us into a conceptual prison.*[3]

Rollins goes further:

> *God hides in God's visibility, realising that revelation embraces concealment at one and the same time as it embraces manifestation and that our various interpretations of revelation will always be provisional, fragile and fragmentary... Even the revealed side of God is mysterious.*[4]

Scriptural References to the Trinity

With Rollins' insight in mind, what can we safely say about the nature of the Godhead? Can we build a picture that avoids the dangers of abstracting and idolising our ideas of God? Karl Barth, who held dearly the view that scripture is inspired by God through human experience, argued that the Bible itself with its many hints and comments about the nature of God actually drives a questioning of that nature[5]. So what are these hints that demand exploration?

For all Muslims, Christians and Jews, experience of God began with Abraham, the root inspiration for all three faiths. God spoke to Abram (as he was originally known), calling him to obedience, to give up everything and leave his own country. Having proved himself faithful to God, a covenant was set up between them. He and his wife Sara both received the letter 'h' in their names as a sign, taken from the name of God, YHWH, of the covenant they had entered into. Muslims cite Ishmael, Abraham's first son, born of Sarah's maidservant Hagar, as the father of their people. Isaac, Abraham's second son, born of Sarah, became the patriarch of the Jews, and Christian's also trace the bloodline of Christ back to Isaac and Abraham through the line of David. The one God thoroughly tested Abraham's faith, most notably through the command to sacrifice Isaac, his only son, born to his wife Sarah miraculously late in life. Abraham's faith, stimulated by his

---

[3] P Rollins, *How (Not) to Speak of God*, (London: SPCK, 2006), 12-16.
[4] Rollins, *How*, 18.
[5] K Barth, *CD I/I*, 295 f, as cited in C Gunton, *Becoming and Being*, (London: SCM, 2001), 127.

testing experiences of God, remained true, and seemed to sustain the faith of those around him. In Genesis Chapter 18 he has a transcendent experience of the divine. The passage describes him becoming aware, through a multi-sensory experience, that the 'one God' was addressing him:

> *The Lord appeared to Abraham ...*
> *Abraham looked up and saw three men standing nearby. When he saw them, he hurried from the entrance of his tent to meet them and bowed low to the ground. He said, "If I have found favour in your eyes, my Lord, do not pass your servant by... Let me get you something to eat, so you can be refreshed and then go on your way – now that you have come to your servant." Very well they answered, "do as you say".* Genesis 18:1-5

From this point on, Abraham's life is transformed as he and his family seek to be obedient to the 'one God'. It marks the beginning of the process whereby YHWH is transformed from being one among many pagan gods, to being Abraham's 'Elohim' – his only God to whom he was committed, and eventually to monotheism – the belief that there is only one God.

This extremely mystical story appears to engage with a God in 'one-ness' yet in three persons. The Lord, the One God appeared in three persons. The story begins with the 'Lord' appearing to Abraham, and then goes on to say appearing as 'three men'. Abraham then addresses the three figures as 'my Lord', appearing to recognise the figures as an authentic manifestation of God. This encounter is never explained, but in Judaism and Islam the story is interpreted as three angels accompanying the invisible God. Christians, particularly from the Eastern Orthodox tradition, see this story as a key point of revelation of God's nature. Andrei Rublev's most famous icon, the Trinity, depicts the scene in the updated, trinitarian context of the Christian Eucharist, but more on that later. For now, this event can be seen as the biblical debut, if you like, of the Christian God, 'One-yet-three'. What should be noted is that God is revealed and experienced in a creative and unanticipated event, not as dry abstraction.

In Genesis there are two renderings of the creation story, the second of which gives us an interesting glimpse into the inner life of God. The text speaks symbolically of a multiplicity on the Godhead.

> *Then God said, "let US make human in OUR own image, in OUR likeness, and let them steward over the fish of the sea and the birds of the air, over the live stock, over all the earth...* Genesis 1:26

It should be noted here that the way Jews and Muslims interpret the Hebrew Scriptures is different. Because Christ made direct reference to it in the gospels, it is celebrated as evidence of the eternally pre-existent Trinity. The language is paradoxical, speaking of Oneness, or 'common-unity' for a number of persons. God, conceived of as the One God, is referred to as a plurality.

Jesus himself, in a spat with the Pharisees makes direct reference to Psalm 110. So significant is the reference, that all three Synoptic Gospels mention it. The text alludes to an inner life of multiplicity in the Godhead:

> *The LORD says to my Lord: Sit at my right hand until I make your enemies a footstall for your feet.* Psalm 110:1 (Also found in Matthew 22:44, Mark 12:36, Luke 20:42-3.)

There are other Old Testament texts that make reference to this 'One God in community'. Many are related with the person of 'wisdom' to the 'creator'. In the Biblical Book of the Proverbs, and the Book of Wisdom in the Apocrypha, there is much focus on the idea and identity of a person called 'wisdom':

> *Does not wisdom call,*
> *and does not understanding raise her voice? ...*
> *The Lord created me at the beginning of his work,*
> *the first of his acts of long ago.*
> *Ages ago I was set up,*
> *at the first, before the beginning of the earth.*
> *When there were no depths I was brought forth,*
> *when there were no springs abounding with water.*
> *Before the mountains had been shaped,*
> *before the hills, I was brought forth—*
> *when he had not yet made earth and fields,*
> *or the world's first bits of soil.*
> *When he established the heavens, I was there,*
> *when he drew a circle on the face of the deep,*
> *when he made firm the skies above,*

> *when he established the fountains of the deep,*
> *when he assigned to the sea its limit,*
> *so that the waters might not transgress his command,*
> *when he marked out the foundations of the earth,*
> *then I was beside him, like a master worker;*
> *and I was daily his delight,*
> *rejoicing before him always,*
> *rejoicing in his inhabited world*
> *and delighting in the human race.* Proverbs 8

The text here is highly symbolic and there is no escaping the identification of the person of 'Wisdom' as a Woman. The language here is so dramatic that both Jewish and Christian traditions have toyed with the interpretation that the feminine imagery is more than just a literary device.[6] Clearly Wisdom is credited with nurturing and creative attributes that need to be taken seriously. The identity of the person of the woman was created, not made. She exists before creation, speaks for Yahweh and lives with him (8:22, 9:10). There is a deep intimacy here between the Lord and Wisdom. She is even described as rejoicing in the presence of the Lord (v30).[7] The encounter is dynamic and playful, and the imagery speaks of participation and co-operation at the creation of the world. The language evokes the imagery of the Genesis creation myths in its use of the symbolism of 'the waters' and 'the deep'. Both 'Wisdom' and 'Word' were present with God before creation, during creation and after creation.

In John's Gospel we find the Word present at Creation, with many references to the Trinity. It opens with a profound statement about the nature of God:

> *In the beginning was the Word, and the Word was with God, and the Word was God. He was with God in the beginning. Through him all things were made; without him nothing was made that has been made.* John 1:1-3

The rest of John Chapter One makes it clear that 'the Word' refers to Jesus the Christ. In this opening chapter the writer of the Gospel of John presents us with a paradox: that Jesus 'was with God' and 'was God' at the same time, and that this was so from the

---

[6] B Edgar, *The Message of the Trinity*, (Leicester: IVP, 2004), 87.
[7] Edgar, *Message*, 90-2.

beginning of creation. He is also portrayed as the Creator of the whole Universe so that 'without him nothing was made that has been made'. Further, he frequently referred to the 'Father' as distinct from Himself, and also discussed 'The Holy Spirit' as a being distinct from either God the Father, or himself:

> *These things I have spoken to you while abiding with you. But the Helper, the Holy Spirit, whom the Father will send in My name, He will teach you all things, and bring to your remembrance all that I said to you."* John 14:25-26

So returning back to the time of creation, Wisdom is seen as a craftswoman, or the perfecter of creation, whilst the Word is identified as the one 'through whom all things were made'.[8] So drawing on this connection between Proverbs, Genesis and John Chapter One we have God the Creator, Wisdom as the Perfecter and the Word through whom all things were made. So God the Creator appears to be dominant at creation, where both the Word and Perfecter are present.

Now the interpretation of these texts has been hotly contested. For some, both the Word and Wisdom have been identified with the person of Christ. Such a view is typical of the Western tradition of thought. Those in the East traditionally make the connection between the female 'Wisdom' and the person of the Holy Spirit.[9] In the very early church the word used for the Spirit was expressed in the female and only later became male.[10] At a later stage we will explore the good reasons why Western theologians may have underestimated the connection between the Spirit and the character of Wisdom, but for now let us hold onto the idea of God participating and co-operating, as having One-ness alongside multiplicity, and as having maternal as well as paternal attributes.

---

[8] Edgar, *Message*, 97.
[9] K Norris, *The Cloister Walk,* (New York: Riverhead Books, 1987), 1. J Hurtak, The Holy Spirit: The Feminine Aspect of the Godhead, (Ava, USA: The Academy of Future Science, 2006), as downloaded on the 9.01.08 on the World Wide Web at
'http://www.pistissophia.org/The_Holy_Spirit/the_holy_spirit.html'.
[10] S G Hall, *Doctrine and Practice in the Early Church,* (London: SPCK, 1991), 41-2, 54-6. J D G Dunn, Spirit, Holy Spirit in D R W Wood (ed..) *New Bible Dictionary Third Edition,* (Leicester: IVP, 1996), 1125-9.

In the first chapter of Luke's gospel we encounter a connection between differing elements of the Trinity. Take for example God's promise to Mary regarding Jesus:

> *The angel answered and said to her, 'The Holy Spirit will come upon you, and the power of the Most High will overshadow you; and for that reason the holy Child shall be called the Son of God.'* Luke 1:35

In this text, Mary's conception is understood as a joint effort of both the Holy Spirit and the 'Most High'. If we count the Son taking form in her womb, Mary has a fully trinitarian experience of God.

In Matthew's gospel in particular, we encounter the three elements of the Trinity as being present at John's baptism of Jesus:

> *As soon as Jesus Christ was baptised, he went up out of the water. At that moment heaven was opened, and he saw the Spirit of God descending like a dove and landing on him. And a voice from heaven said, 'This is my Son, whom I love; with him I am well pleased.'* Matthew 3:16:17 (See also Mark 1:10–11; Luke 3:22; John 1:32)

And again, at the Great Commission, Christ himself talks of God in terms of a plurality of persons:

> *Therefore go and make disciples of all nations, baptising them in the name of the Father and of the Son and of the Holy Spirit, and teaching them to obey everything I have commanded you.* Matthew 28:19-20

In Paul's second letter to the Corinthians we encounter a blessing in the name of a triune God:

> *The grace of the Lord Jesus Christ, the love of God, and the communion of the Holy Spirit be with all of you.* 2 Corinthians 13:13

Not only does this benediction name the Trinity in a blessing, but it also connects an attribute of God with the particular person of the Trinity. Further to this, the writer has created an order that reflects the experience of the believer: that we experience the grace of Christ through the love of God and are then fully able to participate in the divine life of God through the power of the Holy Spirit. Here we encounter what is called the 'economic Trinity', knowing God through what God has done, through the attributes God has self-revealed.[11]

In Ephesians chapter One Paul speaks of his passion for God in terms that are clearly plural. His theology of the triune Godhead comes out of experience of God through worship. It again emphasises an order coming out of experience.

> *Blessed be the God and Father of our Lord Jesus Christ, who has blessed us in Christ with every spiritual blessing in the heavenly places, just as he chose us in Christ before the foundation of the world to be holy and blameless before him in love. He destined us for adoption as his children through Jesus Christ, according to the good pleasure of his will, to the praise of his glorious grace that he freely bestowed on us in the Beloved. In him we have redemption through his blood, the forgiveness of our trespasses, according to the riches of his grace that he lavished on us. With all wisdom and insight he has made known to us the mystery of his will, according to his good pleasure that he set forth in Christ, as a plan for the fullness of time, to gather up all things in him, things in heaven and things on earth. In Christ we have also obtained an inheritance, having been destined according to the purpose of him who accomplishes all things according to his counsel and will, so that we, who were the first to set our hope on Christ, might live for the praise of his glory. In him you also, when you had heard the word of truth, the gospel of your salvation, and had believed in him, were marked with the seal of the promised Holy Spirit; this is the pledge of our inheritance towards redemption as God's own people, to the praise of his glory.*
> Ephesians 1:1-14

Paul articulates God as a Trinitarian community centred on love: we meet God through Christ, who is blessed by God the Father in the power of the Holy Spirit. Here worship is not merely ritualistic action to please a distant God, but an action through which the believer enters into the life of God. It is a personal relationship to and with God the Father mediated by Jesus Christ and perfected by the Holy Spirit.

---

[11] Edgar, *Message*, 35-6.

This statement articulates how Christian worship differentiates from worship of God in the other Abrahamic faiths. It is beyond reciting prayers to a transcendent God outside of the here and now, or of intellectual reflection, it is essentially about invitation to join in the community of the Godhead in the here and now, and be transformed through such an ongoing experience.

In Christianity, worship and encountering the Trinity in the here and now go together.[12] So it is with this Trinitarian idea, that we understand that much of discipleship is centred around a God that is both transcendent and immanent, where God is present in the world, engaging in the world, so that the Christian life is about catching up with what God is already doing.

In the letter to the Hebrews, we begin to hear early formulations for the atonement, or 'at-one-ment', which is about attempting to understand how Christ through the Trinity brings reconciliation between God and humanity for sin:

> *How much more, then, will the blood of Christ, who through the eternal Spirit offered himself unblemished to God, cleanse our consciences from acts that lead to death, so that we may serve the living God!* Hebrews 9:4

Here the trinitarian formulation is used to cast a vision of transformation. Through the crucifixion, death and resurrection of Christ, and the power of the Holy Spirit, we as followers of Christ, are enabled to be free from the consequences and distortions of our own selfishness and self-preoccupation, (which the Christian tradition calls 'sin') through an ongoing and living relationship with the Trinity.

In the first letter of John we find a very strong statement of the co-existing reality of three persons in the one Godhead:

> *For there are three that bear record in heaven, the Father, the Word, and the Holy Ghost: and these three are one. And there are three that bear witness in earth, the Spirit, and the water, and the blood: and these three agree in one.* 1 John 5:7-8

The selections of texts we have explored in this section really help us to see the biblical inspiration for the trinity, and how its formulation, under the circumstances, was quite understandable.

---

[12] Edgar, *Message,* 53-5.

One of the most challenging circumstances for the early Church was the contestation over the nature of the Godhead, and scripture itself was no guarantee of Orthodoxy. One of the first heretics, Arius, made appeal to Scripture for the support of his idea that Jesus had not been fully human. And the Church continued to wrestle with the biblically revealed nature of God for the first five hundred years of its existence. It met in what are now known as the Ecumenical Councils to attempt to bring some coherence to the faith. Some of todays more radically minded Christians see these councils as ending the important role that experience had played in knowing God. However there is clearly a difference between seeking to paint a coherent picture of the nature of God that takes into consideration the entire, varied biblical revelation, and an outright idolatrous objectification that leaves no room whatever for the role of experience. Some believed that Jesus wasn't really human, others that Jesus wasn't really God, and others still that there was only One God and that Jesus and the Holy Spirit were not God, but merely close relatives. Other's saw that Jesus and the Father were related, but not the Holy Spirit. Many were greatly influenced by Greek and Eastern philosophy, which sometimes brought illumination to understanding, but at other times distortion. The early Church Mothers and Fathers had to explore the fragments and hints about Jesus and the Trinity to understand what God had revealed.

The Influence of the Cappadocian Mothers and Fathers of the Early Church

Cappadocia, located in modern day Turkey, was an influential Roman province. It became the stage for a number of highly influential theologians. St. Macrina was the Grandmother and influence to a number of highly important Early Church Mothers and Fathers. These included amongst others; Macrina the Younger (327-379), Basil the Great (329-379), Naukratios the Anchorite (330-357), Gregory of Nyssa (340-394) and their great friend Gregory of Nazianzus (329-379).[13] Together they have become known as the Cappadocian Mothers and Fathers.[14] The letters and theological writings between these family members and friends have been retained by the Church, particularly

---

[13] G.A. Barrois (Ed.), *The Fathers Speak,* (New York: SVP, 1986), 26-30. A Meredith SJ (Ed.) *Gordon S Wakefield A Dictionary of Christian Spirituality,* (London: SCM Press, 1983), 68-70.
[14] *Ibid.*

those of Basil and the Gregories.[15] It is these discussions and explorations that led to the conceptualisation of the Trinity in the early Church articulating a theology of the Holy Trinity that emphasised the distinctiveness of each of the three persons of God.[16] St. Macrina exerted a huge influence upon their thinking. A disciple of Origen had tutored her, and it was her theological education that provided the foundation for her grand children's work. They took it further by utilising the metaphor of image to explain the divine nature of Christ, and to say that the Father and the Son are equal in all things, including being and eternity.[17] God as image is made reference to in the Scriptures, where it says of Christ:

> *He is the image of the invisible God, the firstborn of all creation.*
> Colossians 1:15-17

Rather than closing down meaning and creating certainty, The Cappadocians believed that it was impossible to fully understand the nature of God, and challenged those who proposed such ideas in the early councils. To quote Basil: *'We know the greatness of God, his power, his goodness, his providence over us, and the justice of his judgement, but not his very essence ... we know our God from his operations, but do not undertake to approach near his essence.'*[18] This apophatic approach, which was also infused with the insights of Platonic thought, denies that God's being can be absolutely known or defined. Instead it focuses on the varied and often paradoxical information self-revealed by God in scripture.

So the Cappadocians argued that God has a general, or common essence (ousia), that there are three persons (prosopa) each existing a concrete individuals with their own identities (hypostasis). In nature and being the three are absolutely the same, coeternal and infinite, and utterly distinct from creation, which is finite and exists within time. But they are distinguished from each other by the characteristics of each: the Father is distinguished as the Cause, the Son by being the only begotten, the Spirit by proceeding from the Father. At the time, they went further than other's had before them, by identifying

---

[15] Barrois, *The Fathers,* 15-219.
[16] Hall, *Doctrine,* 156.
[17] *Ibid.*
[18] Hall, *Doctrine,* 157-8.

the Holy Spirit as a person of the Trinity of the same substance and importance as the Father and the Son.[19]

The Cappadocian Trinitarian formulations maintained that despite God's self-revelations, God remains somewhat mysteriously concealed. It further affirmed that God, in God's being, was not static, but something fluid, vibrant and creative.

The implications of perichoresis

Perhaps the greatest gift of the Cappadocians to the Church was the concept of *perichoresis*, which was created by them and developed by St John of Damascus. It draws on two Greek words that do not translate easily into English. 'Peri' has a meaning close to the words 'connecting, surrounding, enclosing, relating in 'close proximity' ', with the sense of being alive and dynamic.[20] 'Choresis' has a meaning close to being distinguishable parts making up something as a whole. The separation of something into two or more parts.[21] Put these two words together, and we have a strong metaphor of something in its 'one-ness' being expressed in dynamic separate parts.

Utilising this concept of perichoresis theologically, it describes the Trinity as three substances, three persons who dwell in one another.[22] 'Peri' creates the sense of dynamism and activity. Here the Creator, Redeemer and Sustainer are interpenetrative, embracing and permeating each other.[23]

This dynamic or fluid understanding of the nature of God has its basis in Johns Gospel, where it says that 'the Father is in the Son and Son is in the Father'.[24] This indwelling expresses and realises a profound sense of fellowship between the persons of the Trinity. The perichoretic relationship is not hierarchical or authoritarian, rather it is characterised by unity in diversity, perfect love, justice and inter-dependency. It describes a God centred in mystery. A God that is both transcendent (outside of here and now) yet mysteriously immanent

---

[19] Hall, *Doctrine*, 158.
[20] A E Laurita, *Greek Roots and Their Modern English Spellings: A Dictionary of Roots Transliterated from Ancient Greek With Their Modern English Spellings*, (New York: Leonardo Pr, 1989).
[21] *Ibid*.
[22] A Walker, *God of the Christians, The Spirit & the Trinity*, (London: HTB Bookshop, 2007), ref: 6374, 6375, 6376.
[23] Gunton, *Becoming*, 232.
[24] *Ibid*. Walker, *Christians*, 6374-6.

(actually here and now). But at the same time, it names a God that only partially reveals the nature of God, through God's actions. No one has ever fully seen God. This understanding does not sell out to certainty, but encourages a sense of a complex and apophatic God, a God slightly out of reach who we will never fully know.

So we meet a God through an apophatic vision of faith and knowing through experience of Gods action in human lives – or what has become called (un) knowing – knowing God through mystical encounter and not knowing God as a set of objectified facts.

In the tradition of the Eastern Church, the perichoresis is known as a dynamic dance in which the different persons of the Trinity lead at different stages in salvation history. The very nature of God is centred on creativity, love and intimacy. A creativity that led to the pouring out of this creative divine love which created the whole Cosmos. All matter both inanimate and the living were therefore created out of the expression of love internally generated within the Trinity and expressed out into the infinity of space and time. So the whole of creation has come out of the inner worship and creativity of God.

John Zizioulas reminds us that this perichoretic understanding of God is that of a being in communion or common-unity.[25] God is seen to model profound devotion to God-self. In Rublev's icon of the Trinity, it is no co-incidence that the persons are engaged in the celebration of the Eucharist. The image perfectly reflects the qualities of perichoresis we have outlined above, and as such it has become very important to many emerging and fresh expressions of church. It is interesting that the Trinity in this understanding has been so neglected in the Western church, particularly within the Reformed stream of theology. To understand more about how we have arrived at this situation, and the significance of it, we must go back to Church history and the ecumenical Councils.

Doctrines & Division
The first three Ecumenical Councils in the early Church were very important for the Christian faith. The first at Nicea (325 CE) addressed what was a coherent understanding of the Trinity. The second at Constantinople (360 CE) addressed the understanding of Jesus as being both fully God and fully human. The final, the Council of Chalcedon (381 CE), affirmed that what had been established at the two earlier

---

[25] Gunton, *Becoming*, 232.

councils were authentic.[26] As was stated earlier, much of the debate was concerned with establishing consistency in the interpretation of Scripture. Many of these heresies were extremely mystical, which might explain why it took the church so long to be able to acknowledge the Holy Spirit as God. In fact as Professor Andrew Walker has said, the doctrine of the Trinity appears to downplay the Holy Spirit somewhat.[27] The doctrine could be criticised as understating the significance of the person of the Holy Spirit. This may have occurred for fear of promoting heresies, which up until the formulation of this doctrine had emphasised the divine nature of Jesus over his humanity. So we are left with a strong sense of the identities of the Creator and the Redeemer, and a somewhat faceless Holy Spirit. However, the doctrine did establish a fresh understanding of the Trinity. The English translation approximates to:

The Creed	*The Attributes*
We believe in one God,	
the Father, the Almighty,	The Father
maker of heaven and earth,	The Creator
of all that is, seen and unseen.	
We believe in one Lord, Jesus Christ,	
the only Son of God,	
eternally begotten of the Father,	The Son
God from God, light from light,	Fully God
true God from true God,	Fully Human
begotten, not made,	The Redeemer
of one Being with the Father;	
through him all things were made.	
For us and for our salvation	
he came down from heaven,	
was incarnate of the Holy Spirit and the Virgin Mary	
and became truly human.	Fully Human
For our sake he was crucified under Pontius Pilate;	
he suffered death and was buried.	
On the third day he rose again	
in accordance with the Scriptures;	

---

[26] Walker, *Christians*, 6375.
[27] Walker, *Christians*, 6375.

he ascended into heaven
and is seated at the right hand of the Father.   Fully God
He will come again in glory to judge the living and the dead,
and his kingdom will have no end.

We believe in the Holy Spirit, the Lord,   The Holy Sprit
the giver of life,   The Sustainer
who proceeds from the Father,
who with the Father and the Son is worshiped and glorified,
who has spoken through the prophets.

We believe in one holy catholic and apostolic Church.
We acknowledge one baptism for the forgiveness of sins.
We look for the resurrection of the dead,
and the life of the world to come. Amen.[28]

      This creed should sound very familiar, as it is recited regularly in many traditions of Church as an act of faith. This doctrine remains widely accepted by the majority of Churches in the East and the West, including the reformed churches. Both Luther and Calvin fully accepted the Nicene Creed.[29] However, it was not plane sailing in the East. A number of Churches, including the Ethiopian and Coptic Orthodox Churches, and the Monophysite Churches, dissented. This resulted in the first great division in the early Church. In the face of significant political pressure, these texts, which were the gift of an ongoing tradition of experience-led revelation of God, became dogma or put another way, became objectified. We must remember that all words we use to understand God are provisional, never definitive, as God can never be fully explained. All revelation of God to humanity is necessarily mediated through human understanding and is therefore subjective. The Nicene Creed, although widely and historically accepted, must be understood as an imperfect human construct. For example, as we will see later, it says very little about the actual life and ministry of the Redeemer. We must be attentive to the Cappadocian Fathers who firmly believed that God could never be rendered fully knowable. We must always honour God's autonomy over all of our ideas about God.

---

[28] Walker, *Christians*, 6375.
[29] Walker, *Christians*, 6375.

St. Augustine's Blunder

Not getting off lightly either, the Western church was also to experience its fair share of division. Augustine of Hippo (354–430 CE), arguably the Father of Western Christianity, put forward an interpretation of the Trinity that has caused complication and dispute ever since.[30] His work was undertaken using a Latin translation of the original Greek text of the Nicene Creed, and he understood God as one substance in three persons (5.8.9)[31] Unfortunately, the translation did not carry quite the same nuance as the original text, and Augustine made the mistake of conceiving of the Trinity as a set of relationships rather than unique personalities or particularities.[32] And therefore he said: *"When it is asked, "Three what?", human speech labours under great difficulty." Nevertheless "Three persons" has been said, not in order to say just that, but to avoid saying nothing'. (5.9.9)*[33] His trinitarianism lacks the perichoretic dimension intended by the Cappadocians, and therefore God became seen in much more static and understandable terms. Many see this as a distinct weakness of Western theology, and as an aggravation of the tension between the East and West. Unfortunately Augustine took this further with the inclusion of the *filioque* clause, added in the West to the Nicene Creed.

He claimed, as others had before him, that the Holy Spirit proceeds from the Father '*and the Son*'. This was not in the original Nicene Creed, and it portrayed the Holy Spirit as subservient to the Son. He failed to see the Holy Spirit as a person at all, and therefore as not equal to the Father and the Son. Photius (c. 820–893 CE) talked of this as a 'down grading' of the Holy Spirit, which made it more of a receiver than an equal person.[34] Colin Gunton (1941–2003 CE) has argued that this downplaying of the Person of the Holy Spirit has created a weakness peculiar to Western theology.

The *filioque* clause was incorporated into the Nicene Creed, in the Western Church, in response to a resurgence of Arianism in the 8th Century. The decision was taken at a Church Council in Toledo, and the revised Creed, which was to become the default option for Western Churches, was used by the Bishop of Rome at a Church service in Rome. This caused a huge row, as no Ecumenical Council had ever

---

[30] Hall, *Doctrine*, 159.
[31] Hall, *Doctrine*, 201.
[32] Walker, *Christians*, 6375.
[33] Hall, *Doctrine*, 201.
[34] Walker, *Christians*, 6375.

agreed to this, which eventually led to the split between the Western and Eastern Churches. It should be noted that there is no biblical justification for the *filioque* clause, and it is counter to a perichoretic understanding of God. We are left with a distorted vision of the Trinity in the Western Church, which has remained as Andrew Walker has stated many times, the Achilles heel of Western Christianity.[35]

The Contribution of Karl Barth
Barth (1886–1968 CE) challenges the static and objectified understanding of the Trinity in the West. He reconnected the Doctrine of the Trinity to a theology of God's self-revelation.[36] In so doing he reinstated a dynamic, perichoretic understanding of God, where God is an event, a happening.[37] God's nature as Father, Son and Spirit is identical to God's nature as Revealer, Revelation and Revealing. And it is in this multiplicity that God's unity consists. He states:

> *If revelation is to be taken seriously as God's presence...then in no sense can Christ and the Spirit be subordinate hypostases...revelation and revealing must be equal to the revealer. I/I 353.*[38]

Under the cloak of modern language, Barth reconnects us with the dynamic God of the Cappadocians. He talks about the being of God as the 'becoming of God',[39] and as such God is understood not as a transcendent thing but as a transcendent happening.[40] God is not eternalised in the past, but seen as the Lord of the future.[41] This is a God of relationships, of three equal persons.[42]

Whilst Barth's approach to the Trinity does challenge Augustine's error, Gunton holds that the significance of the Holy Spirit remains understated, albeit less so than in Augustine's writing.[43]

---

[35] Walker, Christians, 6375.
[36] Edgar, *Message, 90-97.*
[37] Gunton, *Becoming,* 140.
[38] K Barth *I/I 353,* as cited in Gunton, *Becoming,* 139.
[39] Gunton, *Becoming,* 138.
[40] Gunton, *Becoming,* 140.
[41] R W Jenson, *God After God A Study in the Theology of Karl Barth,* (New York: NY Press, 1963), 76, 96 as cited in Gunton, *Becoming,* 140.
[42] Gunton, *Becoming,* 143-4, 229.
[43] Gunton, *Becoming,* 163-6, 233-40.

This weakness of the person of the Holy Spirit in the Western theology, coupled with an overemphasis on the Father and the Son, has led to real problems for the Western Church to which we must now return.

Faith as desire & how (not) to speak of God
The Western Church has long been guilty of an overemphasis on Orthodoxy, or right thinking, to the detriment of Orthopraxy, or right action. Too much significance has been placed on objective truth, which some have argued, distorts faith. I turn to Pete Rollins again:

> *God is not a theoretical problem to somehow resolve, but rather a mystery to be participated in... Religious truth is that which transforms reality rather than that which describes it ... God is not the object of our thoughts but rather the absolute subject before whom we are the object. This is confirmed in baptism when we say that we are 'baptised in the name of the Father, Son and Holy Ghost'. Here we do not name God but God's name names us.*[44]

As a Christian of the Western tradition, I have much experience of the reductive drive to fully know God, of the desire for certainty that distorts faith. The emerging Church, and I would argue the Deep Church movement, recognise the importance of a deeply held Trinitarian theology which counters the superficial drive for objective certainty that boxes God in. Both movements seek a reawakening of the Christian faith as an orientation of the heart, following the unpredictable, dynamic movements of a God who will always elude our desire for control. It is my belief that this ancient:future faith can relate profoundly to a postmodern culture. It challenges us to seek God in the mystery of transcendence, rather than in objectification, to discern God through the experiences of a life of worship that joins in with what God is doing. This Apophatic form of faith seeks understanding, but not certainty, and is happy that we will never fully know God. This is a mature form of faith.

> *When we read that Christ is the truth and that knowing the truth will set us free, we come face to face with truth, not as the objective affirmation of a proposition, but rather as that which*

---

[44] Rollins, *How,* 22-3.

arises from a life-giving encounter. The truth of Christianity is not described it is experienced.[45]

This form of faith has much to with the idea of becoming. First, we encounter in the Scriptures a God that over time begins to self-reveal the divine nature in relationship to human beings. Beginning with Abraham, God 'becomes' in human experience as a transcendent event. Over the course of history people began to articulate their becoming experience of God, which ultimately climaxed in the Nicene Creed and the Triune God. Further, as this God addresses particular human beings, encouraging transcendent spiritual experience, people form expressions of faith arising out of these encounters. Life then becomes a process of human becoming out of this dynamic form of faith. By implication Christ, the image of the invisible God, comes into human history instituting a Christian faith and an emerging form of Church. After Christ, the Spirit as the Counsellor, Sustainer, Companion and Perfecter constitutes an emerging form of Church that grows out of the community of the disciples. Faith comes out of individual experience of the Triune God, and the Church itself is challenged to model itself on the very nature of the 'becoming of God'.

Reflection

The decline experienced by the Western church throughout the period of modernity and now in post-modernity, is due in the main to an inadequate theism. Conceptions of God as one's *best friend*, or as excessively immanent or transcendent, are the result of a failure to accept the validity of, and move beyond, the critique of the enlightenment emancipators. These are still commonly held views, but they do not provide a form of faith that can withstand the cultural and intellectual climate of our times. It is my belief that a trinitarian conception of the nature of God is well suited to the challenge we face in seeking to reconnect people with deep spiritual meaning. In an Age when so many are turned off church by what they perceive as over simplification, we down play the nature of God at our peril.

---

[45] Rollins, *How*, 56.

Chapter Two

Divine (Open) Ended-ness and Transcendence

The penny dropped for me in 1990, in Leeds, in the very early hours one Sunday morning, at a club night called *Devotions*. I had come along interested to know what this "dance night with a spiritual kick" would be all about. For the previous few years I had had a growing sense of attraction toward spiritual stuff in general, and Christianity in particular. It had all started with nothing more significant than a gut feeling that, somewhere out there, was a loving, transcendent force that was on my side. The feeling grew through moving experiences at Easter and Christmas Church services, and a tearful viewing of *Jesus Christ Superstar* on television. Unsurprisingly, given that I had come from an un-churched, unbelieving context, I found that I never quite fitted in at traditional churches. I nevertheless continued to heed the cosmic force that seemed to be beckoning me to come closer. The club night in Leeds was something of a eureka moment. A 'gospel garage' track came blasting out of the speakers, with words about the Three in One God, and of redemptive love, and I was struck by just how full of hope it was. Images were projected on screens depicting the Trinity dancing together, beckoning the onlookers to join in and have a good time. I realised there and then that I was in the awesome presence of a God who accepted and loved me, and that that nightclub had become Church to me, a place of worship. God wasn't bound by four old stone walls, nor was Church. It could be relevant, fun, and participative. The event was put on by the alternative worship group 'Warehouse', now called 'Visions', based at St Michael-Le-Belfry in York. The club in Leeds liked them because their deejaying and veejaying were often better than their secular peers. I went on to be very involved in the life of the Warehouse community, irresistibly drawn by the transcendent sense of the God's presence I encountered there. In whatever they did there was always a strong sense of the Person of the Holy Spirit being present, aside from just God the Father and the Son, a characteristic I had not really encountered before.

When I became a Christian at the age of seventeen, two years before the club night in Leeds, my understanding of God's nature was limited to the deity of Christ. Lip service had been given to the other members of the Godhead, but by comparison with the person of Christ they seemed wholly inadequate. The Father seemed like an old, vengeful man, mostly relegated to ancient history, and the Spirit, something of an impersonal enigma, seemed to operate like the engine of God. The main message I seemed to be getting was that, as the song says, *'its all about you, all about you, Jesus'*. Curiously, in the months following my baptism many of those who were baptised with me began to disappear from the local Church scene. I remember asking one of my newly de-churched friends how this had happened. I'll never forget what he said: *"Well my life got complicated, rough stuff happened, and kept happening. So I began to ask, if Jesus is my friend, why is this happening? I came to believe that Jesus was not my friend at all, as he didn't show it. Jesus gave up on me, so I gave up on Jesus."* This is an all too familiar story, and I have heard it repeated in different forms all over Britain. We are suffering from a very poor understanding of the nature of God, that is unable sustain us in difficult times. As we explored in the last chapter, the Western Church from Augustine onwards has had a weakened understanding of the Trinity, and in particular the Holy Spirit, and this has impoverished generation after generation of Christians in the Western Church.

In my own experience, the Person of the Holy Spirit was often merged with the person of Christ. There was widespread ignorance about the fact of Jesus dependence on the work of the Holy Spirit, visible all throughout the Gospels. Instead the Holy Spirit was watered down to little more than the impersonal engine of God, or the formless wind of God. Walker and Bretherton explain the situation well:

> *The story of redemption can be told as a tale of Father and Son in which the Holy Spirit is neither here nor there. The Spirit can also be expelled from the Godhead through reductionist theologising: even in Pentecostal circles he is sometimes depicted as a 'force field' that emanates from Jesus. The Holy Ghost it would seem is welcomed as power but far less as person.*[1]

In many Churches, the Spirit seemed to act like a magic force, which would be invoked in order to stir congregations up into an ecstatic frenzy. Admittedly, the Holy Spirit does seem to manifest in somewhat unpredictable ways at times, but there is a high price to pay for an impersonal, 'magical force' view of the Holy Spirit, and the correlating hierarchical view of God's nature that results. For example, there is often a strong sense of fear for secular culture, resulting from the belief that the world is utterly fallen, evil and God-less. Preparation for mission activities in the 'outside world' often involves 'praying on' the spiritual armour of God for protection in a society where the same God is otherwise absent. The truth is, that this perichoretic God is fully involved in the world. Looking back at my personal experiences of such Churches, I can see how this entire thinking is based on a profoundly limited understanding of the person of the Holy Spirit. We were aggressive, seeking to argue people into the Kingdom by rational debate, and we had little appreciation for the love of God that was already at work in the world, seeking to restore all things into right relationship. I look back with sadness about how little I knew and how badly I had been taught about the nature of God.

In Chapter One we saw how worship can become mechanical and reductive when it is not seen in the personal, perichoretic context of the Trinity. The same is true with prayer, which is in many churches described as little more than 'telling God' what's on your mind. The Holy Spirit fulfils the function of passing on our spiritual shopping list to God the Father. I have heard it preached from the pulpit that the contemplative forms of prayer are an indulgence, a view I am now completely at odds with. It was said, that prayer is little more than

---

[1] L Bretherton, A Walker, *Recovering Deep Church in Remembering Our Future,* (London: Paternoster, 2007), 13.

'telling God'. This view demonstrates a profound under appreciation of the perichoretic nature of the Trinitarian God. Prayer, like worship, is about encountering and relating with the triune God as an expression of the desires of ones heart. In many churches, intercessory prayer begins with the phrase "in the power of the Spirit and in union with Christ let us pray to the Father". A personal view of the Holy Spirit necessitates a degree of relational maturity on our part, so that prayer comes to involve listening as much as it does talking, giving as much as taking. Contemplative forms of prayer, rather than being an indulgence, are in my view the medium of maturity in prayer and intercession.

Prayer should not be exercised as a power that we have over God, as if God was a heavenly servant at our beck and call, quite the opposite. It is about us learning to 'be' in relationship with and through the divine, a relationship full of mystery and encounter. Nor should it be characterised by the mechanical placation of an angry God, but by grace, love and intimacy. Through prayer we can learn to love as God loves, in powerlessness and humility, and so gain the most profound sense of inner peace. It is through this relational, 'I-thou' approach, that we are enabled to become fully human, going deeper into God and discovering ever more about who we really are.

Worship as Temple appeasement
The temple was for many years the geographical centre of Jewish faith. It was the place where, through the service of the High Priest, atonement was made for the sins of the people. Christians have historically understood that Christ replaced the High Priest, and that he personally atoned for our sin, so that through the power of the Holy Spirit we may find peace with God. A full treatment of the controversies surrounding the various atonement theories is beyond the scope of this book, but what I would like to comment on is the generally accepted notion that Christ has liberated us from the requirement to practise temple worship. What has in fact happened is that the idea of temple worship was reconstituted in the light of Christ's atonement. The New Testament espouses the view that each Christian has become a 'temple of the Holy Spirit',[2] which means that individuals have direct access to God through relationship with Christ. It also emphasises the communal aspect of relationship with God: "when two or more are gathered, I will be there also".[3] Christian worship then is

---

[2] 1 Corinthians 3:16, 6:19, 2 Corinthians 6:16.
[3] Matthew 18:20.

ultimately about our relationship with God and each other, in what the Apostle Paul calls 'the body of Christ'.[4] The highest form of this worship is expressed in Holy Communion or Eucharist, where God is made mystically present through the sacrament to those gathered together. Here worship is the gift of participation through the Holy Spirit in the Son's communion with the Father. Trinitarian worship is about God coming to us and lifting us up.[5] Worship therefore, is centred on God who not only is the object of worship but also leads and inspires the worship at the same time.

Unfortunately for some, Church worship has come to bear a distinct resemblance to Temple worship. Instead of celebrating and encountering the goodness of God, they gather in order to appease the anger of God. Christ has become the Warrior/King God of the Hebrew Scriptures, and is no longer an image of powerlessness, love and grace, but of dominance, wrath and judgement. Worship is something done before God rather than to and with God, a job of work rather than a gift of grace.[6] The emphasis tends not to be on the grace and compassion of God, but on sinfulness and the need for repentance. The resulting guilt that many people experience, is used to clobber them into conformity with the ruling moral norms. Such churches tend to have a weakened understanding of the Trinity, and a belief that God has been rendered fully knowable by revelation. This concept of God is essentially expressing a Unitarian theology, which is, practically speaking, anti-trinitarian.

Mike Riddell, in *Threshold to the Future,* emphasised that such churches seem to have reverted to non-trinitarian monotheism, where the significance of the Trinity as a loving, creative divinity, is somewhat lost. Such Churches tend to have a strict, if unspoken, moral code, and an ungenerous attitude toward human nature, which Riddell calls the 'sin of Holiness'.[7] When we read about Jesus getting angry in the gospels, it is mostly directed at the Scribes and Pharisees. He came down very heavily on them for the absolutising tendency of their faith, which was often dehumanising, oppressive and judgemental.[8] Christ challenges us to live instead by the law of love, which is a reflection of the self-giving deference modelled in the trinity. Holding onto the

---

[4] 1 Corinthians 12:27, Ephesians 4:12.
[5] Edgar, *Message,* 23.
[6] Edgar, *Message,* 22-3.
[7] M Riddell, *Threshold to the Future,* (London: SPCK, 1998), 72-87.
[8] Riddell, *Threshold,* 72-77.

mystery of the God we see there, restrains our oft-felt desire to resolve all mysteries. The result is always a more inclusive, humane expression of faith.[9]

As we noted earlier, many have failed to recognise Christ's dependency upon the Holy Spirit, seen through out the gospels, for the many miracles he performed.[10] While preaching about his own ministry at the synagogue in Nazareth, Christ quotes from the prophecies of Isaiah to highlight the partnership he had with the Holy Spirit:

> *'The Spirit of the Lord is upon me, because he has anointed me to bring good news to the poor. He has sent me to proclaim release to the captives and recovery of sight to the blind, to let the oppressed go free, to proclaim the year of the Lord's favour.'* [11]
> Luke 4: 18-19, Isaiah 61: 1-2

Much Western theological writing has under appreciated this partnership, and lost a sense of the personhood of the Spirit. Ramsey and Terwilliger have challenged this, and proffer the Eastern Orthodox notion of the 'Christ of the Spirit', as an alternative to the Western emphasis on the 'Spirit of Christ'.[12] Here, the life of Jesus Christ is seen as the greatest work of the Holy Spirit:

> *He is incarnate by the Spirit, commissioned at his baptism by the Spirit, driven into the wilderness by the Spirit, empowered in his mighty works by the Spirit and raised from death by the Spirit.*[13]

Seeing the Holy Spirit as a subservient, inferior member of the Godhead, results in a divine, exclusively male, 'one-parent family'. This renders God very susceptible to manipulation by, and as a justification for oppressive patriarchal ideologies. The Spirit contributes many attributes commonly thought of as female, and therefore serves to

---

[9] J Caputo, *On Religion, Thinking in Action,* (London: Routledge, 2001), 92-3, 108.
[10] Matthew 12.23-33, Mark 2:8, Luke 4:14-19.
[11] Luke 4:18-9, Isaiah 61:1-2.
[12] M Ramsey, R E Terwilliger, A M Allchin, *The Charismatic Christ,* (London: DLT, 1974), 7.
[13] Ramsey et al., *Charismatic Christ,* 6, 28-9.

de-gender God. If we begin to see the life of Christ, his wisdom and miracles as the result of co-operation with the person of the Holy Spirit, it opens the way for us to see more clearly the depth of the trinitarian presence of God in scripture. The Spirit is no longer the dynamo or the faceless power of God, but a person of equal stature to the Creator and the Redeemer. We then begin to see that Christ's very ministry modelled participation in the Godhead. This brings real meaning to Christ's call for his followers to join with the Holy Spirit, which he was to send after his ascension. The Church Mothers, Fathers and mystics talk about how the work of prayer involves listening, discernment, and then joining in with what God is already doing. If we are truly attentive to the Gospels, we will not see Jesus himself as the end or goal of our faith. On the contrary, the redeemer always points beyond himself, into the mystery of the Trinity,[14] where the true focus of our worship should be set.[15]

One of the implicit strengths of Trinitarian theology is that God is seen to model unity in diversity. Of course this is largely lost in Western thinking, with its overemphasis on the Father and Son. As a result, much of Western church history can be said to reflect a drive for 'unity in conformity', which has led to some of the worst atrocities and divisions the world has seen. Christ commanded us to strive for the highest form of unity, that of the love of brothers and sisters, so that people would know that he is God.[16] Unfortunately, it seems that the main concern in the West was *orthodoxy,* rather than *orthopraxy.* We therefore have a history deeply marked by schism and disunity, where reform was often undertaken in a divisive spirit, which put right belief before unity. And this is obviously still the case for many Christians. Jane Williams, the wife of the present Archbishop of Canterbury demonstrated this very well in a lecture she gave recently, at St. Paul's Theological Centre in London. She took a bible, and said to those gathered, "Here I have a bible. What would you feel like if I start tearing out pages?" The class looked on horrified, and some responded with cries of "You can't, that's terrible!" Jane continued "So you feel very strongly when I tear out pages of this bible, a book I can buy a replacement for anywhere? How come we find it so easy to neglect and break relationships with other Christians, that once broken, are almost impossible to repair?" Her delivery was passionate and carried the

---

[14] Ramsey et al., *Charismatic Christ,* 24.
[15] Ramsey et al., *Charismatic Christ,* 25.
[16] John 13:34-5.

weight of the conviction she had. The class fell silent, as the uncomfortable truth of what she said sunk in. So often we have put ideas of *orthodoxy* before our love for one another. In the face of the struggles facing the Anglican Communion at present, it is clear she still hopes for 'unity in diversity'.

One of the questions I continue to reflect on is whether the reformation happened in the West because of a poor understanding of the Holy Spirit, with an emphasis on 'truth' and 'freedom' rather than the 'unity' that seemed to matter so much to Christ. A short story will illustrate my point. I went on a short break late last year to stay with a friend in Northern Ireland. On one occasion, while visiting a small scenic town outside of Belfast, I was struck by how many churches could be found on the high street. The Anglican Church of Ireland was a short distance from the slightly younger First Presbyterian Church. A few yards up the road from this, beyond the Second Presbyterian Church, was the actual Reformed Presbyterian Church. At the end of the road was the local charismatic evangelical church. Being such a small town, it was a very sad, very graphic portrayal of the relentless force of reform, and the way in which unity has been taken so lightly.

I have little evidence here to support the hypothesis, but I guess that the aforementioned weakness in Western theology was a significant factor in the precipitation of the Reformation. I also wonder whether the tendency toward institutionalisation in the Western Church is due in part to the lack of a vision of renewal, borne out of an understanding of the Person of the Holy Spirit. It is fascinating that there has not been anything like the same number of reformation movements in the Eastern Church as in the West. This may be due to the relative political instability in the East: the Church leaders were never as powerful as those in the West. Nevertheless, I suggest that the appreciation of the perichoresis of God, and the importance of the Holy Spirit in their theology has helped them maintain the Unity demanded by Christ. I believe that emerging and fresh expressions of Church are rediscovering this understanding, and the space that it opens up for unity in diversity in the 21st century. It is part of a growing discontent for certain elements of our Western theological inheritance, and an appreciation for that of the East. I also believe that the charismatic renewal of the 1960's and 1970s helped to lay the foundation for this rediscovery.

The Charismatic renewal as Trinitarian Correction in the West

The Charismatic renewal arrived in Britain during a period of heightened secularisation and individualism, and its brand of experiential, congregational worship took root quickly. Its influence was felt not only in the independent churches, but the historic denominations too, leading to a radical shake up of evangelicalism.[17] It helped to revitalise the role of women and lay-people in general,[18] whilst also deepening understanding and fellowship between Protestants and Catholics.[19] The inevitable conservative backlash was met head on, and the newfound prominence of the position of the Holy Spirit was retained.[20] Chief among the tools of the new Charismatic movement was a renewed understanding of the trinity. Many naysayers re-evaluated their position in the light of the scriptural assertion of the sovereignty of the spirit: 'the Lord is the Spirit, and where the Spirit of the Lord is, there is freedom' (2 Corinthians 3:17);[21] and when faced with the undeniable freedom with which these Christians worshipped, it was clear that if fellowship were to be maintained, compromises would have to be made. Furthermore, this new spirituality modelled unity in diversity so well, and seemed to be leading to a deeper understanding of the faith that would transcend the divisions of the reformation. Leaders such as David Watson and Michael Harper began to moot the idea that the reformation was in fact a tragedy that could have been avoided, rather than a much needed corrective.[22]

Bretherton and Walker attribute the new insights of what they call the 'deep church movement', to the insights of C S Lewis. In a letter to the Times he wrote:

> *To a layman, it seems obvious that what unites Evangelical and the Anglo-Catholic against the 'Liberal' or 'modernist' is something very clear and momentous, namely, the fact that both are thorough going supernaturalists, who believe in the Creation, the Fall, the Incarnation, the Resurrection, the Second Coming and the ... Last things. This unites them not only with one another, but also with the Christian religion ...*

---

[17] Bretherton, Walker, *Recovering*, 5, 6, 7.
[18] Bretherton, Walker, *Recovering*, 6.
[19] Bretherton, Walker, *Recovering*, 7.
[20] *Ibid.*
[21] *Ibid.*
[22] *Ibid.*

> *Perhaps the trouble is that as supernaturalists ... they lack a name. May I suggest 'Deep Church'.*[23]

Bretherton & Walker attribute Lewis' *via media*, or middle way position, to the work of the Anglican Divine Richard Hooker.[24] As we will explore later, Hooker helped the Anglican Church discover an ecclesiology that would unite both Catholics and Protestants in a single theological framework. The vision was one of unity in diversity, and as we will discover later, very much informed by trinitarianism. Additionally, as Ramsey and Terwilliger point out, the renewal was about more than just unity, and a deepening of the experiential dimension of worship; it encouraged a deeper intellectual engagement too:

> *There is more to the Spirit than being moved, either as individuals or in groups ... we need an intellectual experience of the Spirit as much as an intellectual experience of the Christ. In this enterprise we must return to the sources, to the New Testament, the Fathers and the Eastern Christian tradition, and from all this begin again. We need the Holy Spirit to enlighten us about the doctrine of the Holy Spirit – this will be truly a "new theology".*[25]

Unfortunately the newfound ecumenism was to break down somewhat in the 1970s, succumbing to the factionalism of conservative Anglo-Catholics and Evangelicals. However real change had been achieved, and it was here to stay. Innovations such as 'alternative worship' and the 'emerging Church' grew out of the aspirations of the charismatic movement, with a passion to express worship and community in the context of the 'real world' of consumerism and pluralism. Alongside this, many other charismatic Evangelicals continued to explore the concept of 'deep church'. More recently, the Anglican and Methodist Churches have seen the emergence of 'Fresh Expressions', an initiative that seeks to encourage contextual forms of mission and church. It is clear that a renewed understanding of the Trinity, and in particular of the role of the Holy Spirit, is leading to

---

[23] Bretherton, Walker, *Recovering*, 2.
[24] Bretherton, Walker, *Recovering*, 3.
[25] Ramsey et al., *Charismatic Christ*, 70.

greater innovation and contemporary expressions of Church. So where is all this leading?

Age of the Holy Spirit & the Church

One way of understanding history is as the unfolding story of God's self-revelation. The Creator led the perichoretic dance of God from creation to the coming of the Redeemer.[26] During his ministry, the Redeemer led the dance with participation from the Sustainer and the Creator. Finally, the Sustainer leads from Christ's ascension until the Redeemer comes again. We live in a time of 'now, but not yet', an 'in-between time' when the Kingdom of God has only been partly realised. This is a difficult period for the Church, and relying on the Holy Spirit doesn't guarantee we will get it right, as history has shown. Nevertheless, this time of divine open-endedness, which began at Pentecost, is what Zizoulous describes as the actual constitution of the Church. This is distinct from, and following, the institution of the Church by Christ. The challenge for the Church is to take the nature of its existence seriously, and trust in the guidance and counsel of the Holy Spirit, following wherever God may lead us. The vision for the Age of the Spirit, outlined in II Corinthians chapter 5, is for the restoration of all things into right relationship with God. Each Christian, as a temple of the Holy Spirit, has an ambassadorial role to the world; we are the medium through which the divine mysteriously makes appeal to the cosmos for restored relationship. Teresa of Avila grasped this when she cautioned her fellow Sisters, that when people praise them for their good works, or loving kindness, they were really praising the God that they encountered through them.[27]

Divine (Open) endness & Transcendence

You may find yourself asking, what about eternal life? Isn't heaven the ultimate point of fulfilment in the Christian life? The Cappadocians don't seem so convinced. They seem to have thought that the restoration of all creation into full relationship with the Trinity, or 'theosis', was the end goal of the journey. Their scriptural foundation for such claims lay in the epistles, and such passages as II Peter chapter 2. They argued that such a position was the logical conclusion to St.

---

[26] Where the Creator led, but the Redeemer and Spirit participated. Note: I am not saying here that there was no evolution other than God's hand was in what ever happened.

[27] As recorded in R Williams, *Teresa of Avila,* (London: Continuum Press, 2004), 106-7.

Peter's claim that we will be partakers of the divine nature.[28] That's not to say that we actually become God, but that we will experience the fullness of relationship with the divine for which we had been created, in all of its healed wholeness. This is put beautifully in 1 John 3: 2:

> *Beloved, we are God's children now; what we will be has not yet been revealed. What we do know is this: when he [Christ] is revealed, we will be like him, for we will see him as he is.*

This is not to say that God becomes fully revealed, or that we are to loose the sense of mystery surrounding God's being; rather that we will experience the state of relationship that is the fulfilment of what it means to be human. For those in doubt, another reading of Paul's epistles is encouraged. While I do believe that one day we will live in a restored heaven and earth, I confess that many interpretations of the 'end times' and the afterlife make me deeply uncomfortable. I do not foresee it having overmuch to do with togas, harps, clouds, or grapes; rather I suspect that it will be the fulfilment of what already exists: the restoration of the Cosmos to its potential through relationship with the triune God. Personally, it requires that I trust in the love of God, and continue to journey through life in the hope that I will be drawn deeper into who I am called to be. I am reminded of a story that Mike Riddell told at the Epicentre Network, an alternative worship community in South West London. He was leading a day of exploration into what might help to maintain the spiritual life in the cultural context of Postmodernity. He talked about a profound experience he had had of God in a nightclub whilst out with some friends. The bar was crowded and the atmosphere was vibrant. Many people were dancing. Three people in particular caught their eye. They were quite drunk, cross-dressed men, and they had begun dancing very enthusiastically on top of the bar. On the face of it, this was arguably a most profane, irreverent scene. Nevertheless, Mike recalled having a very profound sense of God's presence in that very moment, it was unmistakable. He was deeply moved by the experience, feeling drawn into a sense of worship, awestruck by something of the beauty of God revealed in these men. Our Trinitarian God likes to mix it up: who's in the Kingdom, who's not; what's a sacred space, what's not, etc, etc. Trusting in this God who loves the marginalised, the sinners, the undeserved and the unlovely, through a profoundly open-ended faith,

---

[28] Bretherton, Walker, *Recovering,* 16.

gives me hope in my own salvation and the salvation of all those I love. It comes down to relational trust in the generous love of the Triune God.

The Trinity & Kenosis
Kenosis connotes the sense of 'giving a gift' or of 'pouring out'. We encounter this 'pouring out' between the persons of the Trinity: the Creator pours out into the Redeemer and the Sustainer, and God 'pours out' love into humanity and the whole of creation. Eastern Orthodox theology emphasises that we are called to follow the example of Christ, and to 'pour out' ourselves in loving others, growing in humility and in union with God, or theosis. This is the process of becoming alike to God, or in fact, developing holiness within us. Kenosis is a concept that provides a deep connection with the wisdom of the sixth and seventh centuries, helping us leapfrog the dry rationality of the Reformation and engage with the Spirit on a transformative experiential level. By pouring out ourselves in the way we see modelled in the Trinity, we share in God's nature and help to bring all things back into relationship with God. It is a great shame that the Church in the West has not understood or appreciated this aspect of God's nature.

Gospel as open-ended and unwritten
None of what I have said so far is beyond criticism. I have followed a particular argument, one that I believe to be true, but which has been greatly criticised by those of a more conservative and Western perspective. One of the most common arguments made against this position is that the gifts of the Spirit were given to the early church to constitute the Church, but then died out once it had become a stabilised institution. How, they argue, have we been able to exist as a church for over a millennium without them? This is arguably a strong position, however, it is weakened for me by the rational, logical and absolute conception of the nature of God that often accompanies it. The resultant beliefs in the inerrancy of the bible, and the cessation of revelation in Christ are very difficult to account for in contemporary society. Such a position recalls the idolatry of the fundamentalist conception of faith talked about in chapter one, where the ideas and symbolic representations for God, become synonymous with God. This diminishes a full understanding of the Trinity because it fails to recognise the role played by the Spirit, and the equality of the person of the Perfector within the Godhead. Trinitarianism preserves the ineffability and mystery of God, asserting that God cannot ever be fully

known. It therefore also guards against the idolising of Scripture. The implication is also that God can change, and we see this in the differences between the Hebrew and Christian Scriptures. The Bible is important within the trinitarian thought, but it not the last word. As history marches on, God continues to work out the divine purpose, and we continue to learn more about that God. In this sense, the gospel can be understood to live within us, as our lives become part of the continually unfolding canon of scripture. We must have confidence in the Holy Spirit to guide and direct us into all wisdom, not to contradict scripture, but to bring new interpretations to light. The Spirit will provide ongoing wisdom and understanding with regard to the many areas the bible does not make direct reference to, and to the few it does. So rather than living in fear, we should have confidence, in all we do, that God is before us, behind us, above us and below us, and that ultimately, our calling is to catch up with what God is doing.

Reflection
In this chapter we have argued that the Western Church has been distorted by an incomplete understanding of the person of the Holy Spirit. We have also suggested that this has resulted in the division we see throughout its history. We have argued that the charismatic renewal, when combined with insights from the Eastern Orthodox tradition, acted as an important corrective to this distortion. These insights have reframed our understandings of prayer, worship, and church and have helped us see what discipleship is all about. They also challenged the idolatry of the fundamentalist viewpoint, and provide for a more complex, transcendental and mystical understanding of the nature of God, where God retains full autonomy.

Chapter Three

Ground of Our Being and Our Becoming through God

A favourite religious movie of mine is Kevin Smith's *Dogma* (1999). One of the early scenes introduces a character that is the epitome of the traditional church leader. He is concerned with plummeting church attendances, attributing them to the Church's failure to engage people with the real person of Christ. He went on to say that the church needed a more contemporary Jesus, a Jesus people could relate to. The resulting character, of which they produce a rather trendy statue, is dubbed 'Buddy Christ', and he smiles, winks and gives the thumbs up. It's an hilarious mock-up of an all too familiar problem: the nature of the person of Christ has always been something the Church has found impossible to reach consensus on. In fact, it is second only to the triune nature of God in the list of befuddling, vertigo-inducing theological chestnuts. Having spoken about the Sustainer in some detail already, we will therefore turn to an exploration of the person of the Redeemer, and after that, to the person of the Creator.

The Nicene Creed conceptualises Christ as having a dual nature, so that he is both human and divine in equal measure. This is patently paradoxical: how can one being be both divine and human? Most of the heresies of the Church were the result of errors in emphasis of either one of these natures. Faithfulness to scripture requires that we appreciate this duality, and see Christ as a 'both and' paradox. Recent Western church history indicates that the balance had tipped in favour of Christ's divine nature. Productions such as *Jesus of Nazareth* (Zefferelli, 1977), and *The Passion of the Christ* (Gibson, 2004) demonstrate this well with their characterisations of Christ as an omniscient, and impassive to the rigours of physical hardship. The image presented here is akin the children's picture-bible portrait of Christ as meek and mild, reverently resting in his transcendent divinity, thinly veiled by his physical body. A truly human Christ could never be so neat and tidy, as we mere mortals can easily testify. He surely experienced the full gamut of emotions and personal crises that the average person would in the passage of their days. I do find it fascinating that so many Christians struggle with the humanity of Christ, and seem to think that even raising questions about it is a sign of irreverence or unfaithfulness. Films such as *The Last Temptation of Christ,* which creatively explores the idea that he was tempted with sexual and relational fulfilment, pose a huge problem for many Christians, many of whom are sure to make their views heard in the media. Personally, I found the film a breath of fresh air, and when it did stray from the biblical narrative it was always to emphasise Christ's human-ness. Denying or trivialising the humanity of Christ constitutes a lack of faithfulness to scripture, and only serves to alienate us from him. Over the course of his life, Christ grew into his true nature; he was, like us, a 'human becoming'.

However, he was no ordinary human being. Indeed, no ordinary human becoming would be so unpredictable, or so mysterious and *other*. In the sense understood within the apophatic tradition, Christ seems to have been impossible to really pin-down, or made sense of. It was easier to talk about what he wasn't. Even though he took the bodily form of a human being, he seemed to play by different rules. This is so much the case that even now, two millennia since he walked the earth we are still trying, and failing, to fully appreciate him. We see this in the way he talked in parables, a literary device which brought new metaphorical meaning to the hearers. Jesus as 'The Word' reflects the character of God. When we speak, we reveal our personality and our character. In this way Jesus is the expression of the immanent God,

God with us, what some have called, the 'Ground of our being'. Jesus was fully human and fully God – 'both and'. But he is never fully knowable, despite what more fundamentalist Christians may believe. Ironically, they are not attending to the Gospel stories, as you cannot hold this position if you actually read the scriptural texts for themselves.

From the dual nature of Christ arise the two great theologies of the Christian faith: Incarnational theology, which emphasises the humanity of Christ, and redemptive theology, which emphasises the divine nature of Christ. In incarnational theology we encounter Christ the servant, the lover of people, who cared for the poor, the children and the marginalised. We encounter the Christ who performed miracles so as to include those excluded from society; essentially, the Jesus that we encounter in the Gospel stories, who is physically present in the World. It has a high regard towards human culture, the need for social justice and the desire to see the Kingdom of God realised in the here and now. It is strong on valuing our common humanity, on inclusivity and the practise of love. Conversely, it has a history of having a low regard towards repentance and obedience. Redemptive theology, which focuses on the divinity of Christ, has a high regard for Christ's call to repentance and to discipleship. It also has a high regard towards Scripture and obedience, conversion and faithfulness, whilst at the same time has tended to have a low regard toward culture, of downplaying our common humanity, human rights and social justice. The image encountered in the book of Revelation of Christ as King, is the predominant conception of God.

These two theologies have divided the Church into Conservatives and Liberals, and Catholics and Evangelicals for centuries, where too great an emphasis has been put on either the divinity or humanity of Christ. The great sadness is that both these theologies are important and true. The Church for centuries has forgotten that we need a 'both and' approach; otherwise we distort not only our understanding of Christ, but also of the Trinity and ultimately of the Church. We will explore later how the emerging Church seeks to correct this, emphasising 'both and', out of a desire to be true to the nature of Christ, and also reflect the Trinitarian foundations of the faith. The irony remains that if the Church is to be true to the full nature of Christ, Conservatives and Liberals, Catholics and Evangelicals, must all stick together. We need to have a high regard towards being human, culture, social justice and inclusion, as well as towards Scripture, redemption, discipleship and repentance.

We must remember the insight of the apophatic tradition, that God will never be fully knowable, and strive not to over simplify Jesus. He will never be our 'best friend'; such a view will never be sustainable, and the truth is much deeper. In his book *The Complex Christ,* Kester Brewin rightly challenges simple solutions to the understanding of the nature of God and the role of Church. He challenges the church to explore afresh what it means to be a 'body of Christ' in the twenty first century. We need to be very careful how we tell the story of God as Creator, Redeemer and Companion, and always maintain the truth that the Redeemer, whilst enfleshed as a human being, was never fully knowable, and so retain the mystery of his person.[1]

Paul Tillich came up with the metaphorical phrase 'ground of our being', to describe the incarnation of God as the Redeemer.[2] This key concept for our postmodern context draws on existential thought, and is a reaction against a faith that had become objectively certain and described in absolute terms. Existentialists believe that human beings define their perception and understanding of the world from experience, distrusting empiricism and approaches focusing on absolute truth. They believe that reality transcends scientific approaches. So Tillich advances the metaphor of Christ informing our identity as the 'ground of our being', thereby emphasising the immanence of Christ. Therefore, as Tillich would have it, we ultimately perceive reality through the experience of God.

Stuart Murray is one of many writers to have commented on how the Nicene Creed jumps from the nature of Christ's birth to his death, saying very little about his life.[3] He argues that the profound teaching Jesus gave concerning how we should live has not been emphasised, particularly regarding the challenging of injustice and meeting the needs of the poor:

> *The Nicene Creed, for instance, says Jesus 'was incarnate by the Holy Ghost of the Virgin Mary; and was made man. And was crucified also for us under Pontius Pilate.' It ignores his human life, moving straight from his birth to his death. Where*

---

[1] K Brewin, *The Complex Christ,* (London: SPCK, 2004), Chapters 1-3.

[2] P Tillich, *Systematic Theology Volume One,* (London: University of Chicago Press, 1973), 116-7, 155-8, 234-6. R M Pomeroy, *Paul Tillich: a theology for the 21st century,* (Lincoln: iuniverse, 2002), 1, 12-3, 22-30.

[3] S Murray, *Post-Christendom,* (Carlisle: Paternoster, 2004), 123-124.

> *are his miracles, relationships, teachings or subversive lifestyle? As in many fourth-century documents, where is Jesus? The other creeds contain this same startling omission.*
>
> *Explanations can be offered - creeds cannot include everything and the human life of Jesus was not something fourth-century theologians were debating, so this was not included. But this is precisely the point: Jesus' life and teaching were no longer the focus of attention. Christendom [church] was comfortable with a divine Jesus - and with belief that Jesus was also human - but struggled with the challenging reality of that human life. Though the creeds declare his humanity, this seems little more than an abstract philosophical principle ... Jesus was worshipped, but not followed. This has left a lasting legacy ... Jesus [as human] was consigned to the margins.*[4]

The incarnate Redeemer challenged the rich young man, the might of Rome, the powers of the Jewish Temple and its Priests, with another way of being. We see this explicitly with his suggested civil disobedience concerning the Roman Army. When asked about what to do when a soldier hits you, Jesus recommendation of offering the other cheek is politically subversive, because it would force the Roman Soldier to hit you with the inside of their right hand, and thereby acknowledge you as their equal. Further, when Christ directs his disciples to take the soldiers pack and extra mile, he is also being subversive, because it was illegal for a Roman Soldier to ask this. There is much more in the Sermon on the Mount that is profoundly challenging and political. So when someone says that you should never mix Christianity and politics, you will need to challenge them. It may not be in the Nicene Creed, but it is very much part of our calling to follow the way of the human Christ as believers. The Christian Faith should relate to how we live, not just to what we might think. In the words of the Redeemer we find direction as to how we should live, consistent with a radical yet loving form of discipleship that has a high view of justice and inclusion, modelled on the perichoresis.

Implications of the Creator
One of the great tragedies of Western thought is its understanding of the relationship of God with humanity and creation. Traditionally

---

[4] *Ibid.*

Genesis chapter 1 is interpreted as God giving humanity the right to subdue creation rather than be stewards of it.[5] This has progressed to an understanding that creation is little more than a resource, something to utilise. There has been a general lack of understanding of the important connection between creation and the creator. Since the Enlightenment, the most common understanding in the West was that God was a kind of 'watch maker', who set the Cosmos going and then stood back for a long time, only to reappear briefly in Christ.[6] The danger of this position is that it validates the view that the created order is little more than 'dirt', and has no spiritual value. There is an acknowledgement that creation shows something of the handiwork of the creator, but little more.

The Eastern Church frowns on this position, believing that God, as the Holy Spirit, is transcendent and other to creation, but at the same time present to sustain it in its being. In this view God is not of creation, but is present to creation. The Eastern Churches have a more *panentheistic* theology, where God is understood to be omnipotent, eternal and other, and yet present in all creation, enabling it to exist. Put another way, God's energy maintains all things and all beings, even if those things have explicitly rejected God. Because of God's love for creation, God does not remove the divine presence from it. (As an aside, this is not the same as *pantheism*, which says that creation is all that God is.) So rather than creation being just dirt, there is a mystical relationship between all matter and the divine. Thus, once more we meet the Holy Spirit, sustaining all life and matter in partnership with the Creator and Redeemer in the perichoretic dance of God. God is seen as the 'affect and effect' of the Universe, and as with perichoresis, the interpenetrative Trinity also interpenetrates every part of nature, and timelessly extends beyond as well. It has been somewhat impossible for Western theology to go this far as it has not had a developed understanding of perichoresis or of the role and person of the Holy Spirit. Only with these in place could panentheism be understood.[7] It could be argued that we in the West have plundered creation through a

---

[5] P Harrison, *Subduing the Earth: Genesis 1, Early Modern Science, and the Exploitation of Nature* The Journal of Religion, Vol. 79, No. 1 (London: University of Chicago Press), 86-109.

[6] J Zuck, *Biblical Panentheism,* as downloaded from the World Wide Web 11.02.2007 at 'http://www.frimmin.com/faith/godinall.html'.

[7] R Totten, *The Worldview of Panentheism,* as downloaded from the World Wide Web 11.02.07 at
'http://www.geocities.com/worldview_3/panentheism.html'.

diminished understanding of the connection between creation and the creator, and only now, in a time of acute environmental crisis are we waking up to the importance of ecological stewardship and justice. Only now are we beginning to understand scriptural texts that talk of all creation groaning and waiting for redemption.[8] The Cosmos has a touch of the sacred, reflecting the awesome beauty of the Creator who continues to sustain it, despite our best efforts to destroy it. This is not dodgy theology as argued by some conservative theologians; on the contrary, it is another aspect of the Christian faith that has remained underdeveloped in the western church. The environmental crisis we face has helped western theology to catch up with some of the thinking prevalent in Orthodox theology. I hope never again to see Christian environmental campaigners be labelled as dodgy liberal do-gooders again. It is quite reasonable to be moved by the beauty of creation, and as a keen surfer I find it easier to worship God in the midst of the beauty of the ocean and the coast, than I do in most churches. I am constantly moved by a sense of God's Trinitarian presence in nature. This natural revelation is also an important stepping-stone for people to encounter the living God. Although, to my distress, many Christians still fail to see the connection between faith and environmental stewardship, the emerging church, alternative worship, and deep church movements do seem to have gained, and recontextualised some insights from the Eastern faith tradition. This is beginning to change our behaviour in that we are starting to seek ecological and environmental justice through stewardship. It is my hope that this will eventually affect global politics. We need it very soon!

    We are invited in worship, by implication, to join in and participate with the Creator, Redeemer and Companion and therefore also with all created matter. We join in with God, and the whole universe, in a truly cosmic understanding of Christian worship. Many alternative worship groups have experimented with this idea in Eucharistic liturgies, drawing inspiration from the created, sacramental realm, to make God present through the bread and wine. Their mystical services, entitled, for example, 'Cosmic Eucharist' or 'Creation Eucharist', have been opening up this whole area as an authentic expression of Christian worship. This has been an important innovation in an age of increased interest in spirituality and mysticism.

    This form of worship is not just about encounter with God, it is profoundly about how we live. One way of reinterpreting Genesis

---

[8] Romans 8:22.

Chapter One is as God making a covenant with humankind, so that we become the stewards of the Universe. Covenants were ancient agreements between people groups that were eternally binding, and included ceremonies where people became 'blood brothers' by cutting each other and sharing each others blood as a sign of commitment. This is where we get the idea of the Old Covenant or Hebrew Covenant, and for Christians, the New Covenant in Christ. If Genesis chapter One can be interpreted as a Covenant, then our worship of God should include how we behave towards creation. In this way recycling, using renewable energy, getting rid of your car, are all authentic expressions of worship. Worship of God is about how we live as well as the more mystical and transcendent elements.

Finally, I want to make some links between all that we have learnt so far. We see that the Holy Trinity is an interpenetration of the three persons of the One God, a dynamic, perichoretic relationship, the outworkings of which are love, perfect justice and inclusion. Therefore, the Kenotic 'pouring out' of God from the Creator to the Redeemer and the Spirit is shared not only with us, but also with the whole of creation. God can therefore be understood to interpenetrate and sustain all creation in a panentheistic manner. There is a deep connection between these concepts, whose common root is the Creator within the Trinity. It is in the Creator, that Perichoresis, Kenosis and Panentheism find their root in the context of the Trinitarian God. There is deep symmetry here theologically, something we in the West are still learning about.

Knowing through the Spirit
We have already extensively explored the implications of the person of the Holy Spirit in Chapter Two, but there are a few more things to say. We have called the Holy Spirit the perfecter of our faith, but how does this work in practice? How does the Holy Spirit perfect things? I want to argue here, that imagination is very important and that we need a theology of the imagination, where insight is gained from an emerging sense of spiritual experience. When you think about it, when we pray and when we worship, we do actively engage our imaginations. This is evidenced by the sense of awe and transcendence we occasionally experience. Imagination can be the meeting place between the Holy Spirit and us. You could argue that committed forms of spiritual reflection are about being open minded and open to the promptings and insights of the Holy Spirit. This is why John Taylor in his famous book called the Holy Spirit the 'Go-Between God', who draws and beckons us to reimagine what is possible or re-encounter God through

promptings. Our imagination becomes the place for seeing new potential and new concepts, as well as the place where we meet and encounter God through the Holy Spirit. The parables used by Jesus illustrate this point well. They have deep metaphorical meaning and encourage us to understand through enabling us to re-imagine. This is understanding through experience, or knowing God through experience of God, as opposed to knowing God through facts. This form of knowing will always be emerging because new knowledge or language comes out of the interplay of the Holy Spirit with our imagination and experience. It is in this profound way that we are led into new understandings, new appreciations. Some of this approach does exist within the history of the Western Church, principally through the Quaker tradition. They do not give sermons in the traditional style, but waited together for the Holy Spirit to speak through various individuals, in the form of thoughts, images, or impressions upon their imaginations. This is not unlike what happened at some of the Charismatic services I have experienced. It is easy to mock, but I do like the open-endedness of this approach, seeking the involvement of the Holy Spirit. It doesn't have to look so wacky either. Deep theological reflection can be open to this just as much as that which is more emotional.

Many books, including Kester Brewin's, have focused on the idea of 'emergence' and the 'emergent'. Brewin's book focuses on this metaphor for Church as the 'body of Christ', and argues that these 'bodies of Christ's' are distorted by hierarchical forms of leadership and by having professionally paid workers, including priests. For Brewin, Church should be a community of participation, with flat leadership structures. I cannot agree with all of this, but he is right to desire a church that is participative and that fully reflects the perichoresis of the Trinity. What I find particularly fascinating about his book is that he challenges the church to look at the organisation that occurs in nature. For example, ant nests were thought to be top down organisations, but really they are self-organising, emergent communities, where different individuals are given different roles. He points out that cities too, operate under processes of self-organisation, and no one person is in control of movement or of where people work. He considers it possible for the church to become a self-sustaining emergent organisation as seen in nature. A panentheistic theology of nature indicates that there is something of God's hand in these natural organisations. Such organisations can be understood to find their dependency on the Holy Spirit so as to be able to form self-sustaining emergent communities. The great advantage of this could be the empowering of the 'people of God', the laity, to be the church, moving away from passivity and 'church going' to 'church being'. It is still possible to be this form of church, with division of labour and specialisation, where people are given leadership roles but where all are equal, as a form of flat leadership. The main advantage of this for the church is the shift from being an institution, back to being a community. The main disadvantage appears to be that you can only do this with a limited number of people. Nevertheless, if we are sincere about seeking ways of being church as community, there is a lot of wisdom in what Brewin is saying.

All of the various church movements since the Reformation started out as a movement of the Spirit, and a desire to live out an expression of church that was more communitarian and participative. Although I think the division caused by the Reformation is regrettable, I sense that many were driven by God to seek a more perichoretic understanding of God, with Church as participative, having flat leadership and far more of a vibrant community. It may be that it is the Holy Spirit that seeks to retain the sense of a participative community in the church, and so limit the tendency toward institutionalisation. This is something I think the Holy Spirit still beckons the church to be today.

The Emerging Church And the Holy Spirit
There has been much written on the Emerging Church and I cannot hope to summarise it fully here. I will say that I consider it to be an authentic expression of Church that seeks to be contextual, participating fully in the more postmodern aspects of culture. What is of key interest here is whether it is a genuinely Holy Spirit-led reconstitution of Church for a new expression of culture. Many of the people I have known who have been involved in the emerging Church, have come from some experience of the Charismatic tradition. While many still have a strong understanding of the Holy Spirit's participation in the world and their lives, they are progressively more mystical in that understanding. The beginnings of the emerging Church suggest that it may be such a Holy Spirit led innovation. Murray identifies 'emerging churches' beginning in the Late 1990s as:

> *An apparently spontaneous phenomenon...without central planning, coordination, or consultation. Loose networking, shared stories, 'blogging' on websites and developing friendships were all that connected otherwise isolated*

initiatives...The churches that have emerged in the past few years have been remarkably diverse ....[9]

Many emerging churches ... were not intented to become churches but developed into churches as those involved found their ecclesiology transformed by engagement with the community they were serving ... They grew into churches as those involved found the culture gap between new Christians and church too wide....[10]

For some Emerging Churches, there is a temptation to be defined by what they are not. However, for a number there is a real Trinitarian basis to their identity, and as such they are spiritual communities that reflect the need for participation, creativity and inclusion. One of the first books written on the emerging church by Larson and Osbourne sets out a clear vision for a focus on 'unity in diversity', with a 'both and' mentality that seeks to reverse the fragmentation of the church.[11] It is therefore a synthetic style of church, drawing on both incarnational and redemptive theologies. Larson & Osbourne note the following themes:

- Rediscovering contextual and experimental mission in the western church.
- Not restrained by institutional expectations.
- Open to change and God wanting to do a new thing.
- Use of the key word "and". Where the heady polarities of our day seek to divide us into an either-or camp, the mark of the emerging Church will be its emphasis on both-and. For generations we have divided ourselves into camps: Protestants and Catholics, high church and low, clergy and laity, social activists and personal piety, liberals and conservatives, sacred and secular, instructional and underground.
- It will bring together the most helpful of the old and the best of the new, blending the dynamic of a personal Gospel with the compassion of social concern.

---

[9] S Murray, *Church after Christendom,* (Carlisle: Paternoster Press, 2004), 69-70.
[10] Murray, *Church*, 74.
[11] B Larson, R Osbourne, *The Emerging Church,* (London: Word Books, 1970), 9-11.

- It will find its ministry being expressed by a whole people, wherein the distinction between clergy and laity will be that of function, not of status or hierarchical division.
- Due emphasis will be placed on both theological roots and contemporary experience, on celebration in worship and involvement in social concerns, on faith and feeling, reason and prayer, conversion and continuity, the personal and the conceptual.[12]

If this is truly the vision behind the emerging Church and the Deep Church movements, and the driving force in the Fresh Expressions movement, then it may also be truly of the Spirit, who desires to perfect us and draw us back not just into restored relationship with the divine, but to restored relationships with other Christians.

Reflection: Visual expression of the Trinity

Now I have used a lot of words so far to articulate an understanding of the Holy Trinity as Creator, Redeemer and Sustainer. It is time now to explore this visually. On page 64 is a Greek copy of Rublev's ikon of the Trinity, which is centred on the mystical story of Abraham and the three angels. After reading the explanation below, I invite you to sit with the ikon as an act of worship with God through the image. To be able to see a colour copy of this ikon on your computer through the internet, go to "http://www.moot.uk.net/the-becoming-of-G-d".

The image reflects the story in Genesis of the encounter between Abraham and the three Angels that mysteriously become God. The image begins with the three persons as Angels, hence the wings. This is important, as according to Orthodox tradition, it is somewhat idolatrous to image the Creator who remains unrevealed.

In the centre is the Creator God. Behind this person is the Tree, signifying creation, the tree of life, and also the tree of death. Sitting to the right of the Creator is the Redeemer, to whom the other members of the Trinity bow their head in respect. Behind the Redeemer is the tower of Babel, signifying humanities rebellion against God. On the other side of the Creator is the Sustainer, who is coequal with the Creator and the Redeemer. Behind the Sustainer is Mount Sinai, the place where Abraham was tested with the potential sacrifice of his son Isaac. It is also the place of the temple and of Jerusalem. Before the great symbols

---

[12] Ibid.

of the Hebrew Covenant we meet the Holy Trinity, expressing oneness. They model perfect love, justice and inclusion. As you look at their faces for a minute, imagine the kenotic pouring out of God into God-self. This ikon is incomplete until you recognise that you are being beckoned to join with the three persons of God, relationally, and as an act of worship. Finally, in front of the perichoresis of God, we encounter the symbols of the New Covenant of God. In ancient tradition, the bread is already mixed into the wine, in the cup. So finally this ikon draws you, through the sacraments, into worshipful relationship with the divine tri-unity. Just like everyone before, the ikon draws you to worship God so that you join with the whole timeless communion of Saints. Look at the feet. They are poised for movement, as if preparing to dance. This is not a God that sits still. Our challenge is to keep up with this God. So sit with this ikon for a while.

(c) Ian Mobsby and Tim Dendy

Chapter Four

Models and Lessons from the Emerging Church

In 2005, I completed research exploring how emerging churches operating within an Anglican context were being authentically church. It became immediately obvious that Rublev's ikon, *Trinity,* was immensely important for all four of the emerging Church projects I spent time with. It was used as a visual image incorporated into event flyers, or for alternative worship meditations, or just in the general worship life of the various communities. Further, it was found in offices, over work desks, in homes, everywhere, in fact. It was clear that it was bringing profound theological and social meaning to those involved in the various projects. Two of the projects opened all their services with an invocation to the Holy Trinity. Whether they were conscious of it or not, a developed Trinitarian understanding of God was evident in this worship. As I looked deeper, it became clear that all the groups I was researching appeared to have a profound understanding of the Trinity which was informing how they were church, where church is understood functionally as the activity of worship, mission and community.[1] All the groups had a strong sense that mission was about

---

[1] See my book I Mobsby, *Emerging & Fresh Expressions of Church*, (London: Moot Community Publishing, 2007).

catching up with what God was already doing. Many of them were engaging with spiritual tourists, and in so doing, sought the presence of the Trinity in unlikely places. One of the most profound examples of this, which took place at many Mind, Body and Spirit Festivals, concerned the exploration of the Trinity through the imagery of tarot cards. All the groups had a profoundly Ancient:Future focus which was refreshing and invigorating. They believed that the triune God was present in all parts of life, and in all places. There was a strong sense of the Person of the Holy Spirit being present as the Companion and Sustainer, something you do not hear much of in many western churches. Further, some of the groups articulated a profound desire for a model of church that reflected the relations of the Trinity as a participative and creative community.

For my first book, *Emerging & Fresh Expressions of Church*[2] (the compilation of my MA research dissertation) I interviewed a number of emerging/Fresh Expressions of Church to explore how their ideas of 'being church' compared theologically and sociologically. A year later, Eddie Gibbs and Ryan Bolger produced the book *Emerging Churches*, drawing from a PhD thesis on the emerging church and a collection of personal stories, including my own. They interviewed a great number of emerging church projects in Europe and the USA, all of which held the same core seven values. Many of those involved had never personally met, other than through websites and blogs, so it was astounding that there was so much consensus. The values of the emerging church were identified as:

1. *Who take the life of Jesus as a model to live (life as spiritual journey).*
2. *And who transform the secular realm.*
3. *As they live highly communal lives.*
4. *Welcome those who are outsiders.*
5. *Share Generously.*
6. *Participate.*
7. *Create.*
8. *Lead without control (unity in diversity).*
9. *And function together in spiritual activities.*[3]

---

[2] Mobsby, *Emerging,* 50-68.
[3] E Gibbs, R Bolger: *Creating Christian Communities in Postmodern Cultures*, (London: SPCK, 2006), 44-5.

I was given the opportunity to reflect on these findings when Ryan Bolger presented them to a gathering of emerging church leaders in the UK. I asked those gathered the question: "Where do these values come from? How has so much consensus been reached?" I then suggested that perhaps the Emerging Church had found, or been led to a Trinitarian ecclesiology which had inspired a model, the values of which reflected God's desire for what the emerging church should be. This is what Volf is talking about in *After our Likeness*. A Church whose values reflect the Trinitarian God.[4] This development appears not to have been a consciously mediated action, but to have emerged out of the experience and practice of those involved in the projects. Is this a God-led re-imagining of Church? Personally, I believe there is too much of a coincidence to say otherwise. If you look at these values for just a minute, they very much speak of a church modelled on perichoresis and kenosis.

Value One: following Christ as a model of discipleship. This connotes the sense of *human becoming*, discipleship, and Church as a group of disciples seeking to live out together what Christ called us to live.

Value Two: the transformative pouring out of God from the sacred into the secular. The Church reflects this call to worship God and in so doing, pours out itself in loving action mixing up the sacred and secular in the pursuit of transformation drawn from the love of God.

Value Three: as God lives in perichoresis, belonging and love, so the church is called to express community, belonging and mutual love.

Value Four: practicing hospitality. As the Holy Trinity draws people into relationship with the divine, so should the church seek to love and draw into relationship those outside of itself.

Value Five: as the perichoretic Triune God interpenetrates itself in participation, love and inclusion, so the Church should be a generous, sharing community.

---

[4] M Volf, *After Our Likeness: The Church as the Image of the Trinity*, (Cambridge: Eerdmans, 1998), 191-220.

Value Six: as with God's perichoretic nature, where the three persons participate in God's oneness, so should the church participate and include everyone as an expression of the Church's oneness.

Value Seven: as God creates and sustains the cosmos and inspires human development, so the Church should encourage creativity and development in all those involved.

Value Eight: as the Trinity models unity in diversity, where all three persons are co-equal, so should the church reflect the sense of being a body of co-equal persons in one community.

Value Nine: as the Holy Trinity playfully and dynamically engages with the Cosmos, so the Church should in its togetherness, host spiritual activities.

In short, these values appear, to me at any rate, to be informed by a trinitarian ecclesiology whether people are aware of it or not, and it is probable that the use of Rublev's Ikon brought deep theological meaning, modelling an expression of church to which they all aspired.

What is driving these values?
So if I am right, and I believe that in this area I may be, the Holy Trinity is beckoning the emerging Church to model a way of being a spiritual community that reflects the very nature of the Trinitarian Godhead. The Holy Spirit is drawing those seeking missional and contemporary expressions of church for our postmodern consumerist context, to experiment with forms of church drawing on a perichoretic model. As an aside, I remember that I first encountered the theological significance of Rublev's ikon at a worship event led by Dr Luke Bretherton, where he led a meditation on it. Luke is now one of the key contributors to the Deep Church movement. Further, in a lecture by Prof. Andrew Walker of Kings College, London, to Ordinands at St. Paul's Theological Centre, the ikon was used to illustrate the meaning of perichoresis. Andrew is also key player in the Deep Church movement. Therefore, I now think that this Ikon may also have opened up a whole depth of meaning, not only to the Emerging Church network but also to the Deep Church movement. I love the idea that this ikon may be the Holy Spirit beckoning us on, transforming our imaginations, and helping us re-imagining another way of being. Taylor puts this eloquently:

> *Any attempt to image God contextually is in fact an act of God reading us. As we embody God, as we proclaim God in community, God looks back, questioning the church: Is the church fully representing the image of God? Is the church a participatory place where people find their full humanity in Christ? Is the body of God a true ikon of God?...Will we let the image of God construct us?*[5]

It is clear that this form of thinking, of a Church reflecting the nature of God, has highly influenced a number of writers involved in postmodern theology or ecclesiology. As Tillard and Grenz write:

> *Ultimately then, we enjoy the fullness of community as, and only as God graciously brings us to participate together in the fountainhead of community, namely, the life of the triune God...The community that is ours is nothing less than shared participation – a participation together – in the perichoretic community of Trinitarian persons.*[6]

> *In the end, participation in the perichoretic dance of the triune God as those who by the Spirit are in Christ, is what constitutes community in the highest sense and hence marks the true church...*[7]

But is this scriptural? I hear you cry, this concept of the Church modelled on the nature of the Trinity? Volf argues that this form of Church as participation in the communion of the triune God, (which brings hope and present experience), has a strong New Testament basis. Further, he implies that this concept of church appeared to 'emerge':

> *New Testament authors portray the church, which emerged after Christ's resurrection and the sending of the Spirit, as the anticipation of the eschatological gathering of the entire people of God...The eschatological fulfilment of the high-priestly prayer of Jesus, (John 17:21) I ask...that they may all be one.*

---

[5] S Taylor, *The out-of-bounds church? Learning to create communities of faith a culture of change*, (Grand Rapids: Zondervan, 2005), 71.

[6] J M Tillard, *dilemmas of modern religious life*, (Delaware: Michael Glazier, 1984) in S J Grenz, *Ecclesiology* in K J Vanhoozer (ed.) *The Cambridge Companion to Postmodern Theology*, (Cambridge: CUP, 2003) 268.

[7] Grenz, *Ecclesiology*, 268.

> *As you, Father are in me and I am in you, may they also be in us.*[8]

Furthermore, the mutual giving and receiving in such a mystical community is modelled on the Trinity, which is mutually abiding and interpenetrative:

> *So that you know and understand that the Father is in me and I am in the Father (John 10:38, 14:10-11, 17:21).*[9]

Volf also argues that the church prefigures, albeit dimly, the eventual eschatological restoration of all creation into relationship with God (1 Corinthians 12:4-6).[10] So there is a strong New Testament basis to this form of Church. To explore this further we must turn to the work of Avery Dulles.

Models of Church

In his key book, Dulles explores a number of different models of Church, from across the various denominations, each reflecting various aspects of the nature of God, and of Christ in particular. It is my view that the models corresponding most accurately to the normal functioning of the emerging Church are the 'Mystical Communion Model' and the 'Sacramental Model'.[11] This is borne out by the qualities of Rublev's ikon, which we have seen is so important to the emerging Church community. It not only models the Kenosis and Perichoresis of God, but is also set in the context of the sacrament of Holy Communion. Let's explore both of these models in greater detail.

Mystical Communion Model

This model of church is centred on a sense of community that reflects the Godhead in perichoresis. Church then is more of an interpersonal community rather than an institution. It is a fellowship of participating individuals, brought together through God and in particular through Christ. The "I thou" relationship with God is a gift of Grace, rather than a demanding one of obedience and good works. The model connects

---

[8] M Volf, *After Our Likeness: The Church as the Image of the Trinity*, (Cambridge: Eerdmans, 1998), 128-9.
[9] Volf, *After* 208.
[10] Volf, *After*, 235.
[11] A Dulles, *Models of the Church,* (New York: Doubleday, 2002), 39-54, 55-67.

strongly with the mystical 'body of Christ', a communion centred on the spiritual life of faith, hope and charity. The model resonates strongly with Aquinas' notion of the Church as the principle of unity that dwells in Christ and in us, binding us together and in God. It consists of equal persons drawn together to spiritually journey with one another in God. Mission becomes the activities that dispose people to an interior experience of belonging and eventual union with God effected by grace.[12]

Dulles sees this form of church as empowering its members to fully participate in the life of the spiritual community, as they are animated by supernatural faith and charity, and led into communion with the Divine.[13] Because of its fluidity, Dulles believes that this form of church is good at adapting and responding to social change. Regarding traditions of church, this model is open to both Protestant and Catholic:

> *In stressing the continual mercy of God and the continual need of the Church for repentance, the model picks up themes of Protestant theology...[and] in Roman Catholicism...when it speaks of the church as both holy and sinful, as needing repentance and reform...*
>
> *The biblical notion of Koinonia...that God has fashioned for himself a people by freely communicating his Spirit and his gifts...this is congenial to most Protestant and Orthodox... [and] has an excellent foundation in the Catholic tradition.[14]*

It is therefore unsurprising that this framework enables Church to reflect the 'both and' vision of the Emerging Church, drawing on the best of the Catholic and Evangelical traditions in a new, or should we say 'old' synthesis. It is an expression of faith that reflects the relational and mystical quality of the spirituality arising out of the postmodern elements of our culture. We will look at this more closely in the next chapter.

There are also however a number of disadvantages to this way of being church. Firstly, because of its organic nature, it can be difficult to define where church begins and end. There is a danger of over

---

[12] Dulles, *Models* 44-53.
[13] Dulles, *Models*, 50.
[14] Dulles, *Models* 46, 50-1.

spiritualising and deifying the activity of this type of church. If the Holy Spirit were conceived of as the life principle of the Church, then all actions of the church would seem to be attributed to the Holy Spirit. This obscures the personal responsibility and freedom of the members. In such situations there could arise issues relating to the abuse of power, resulting in unhealthy forms of community.[15] The greatest weakness of this model is that it can undervalue the significance of Christ as a human being, where everything becomes too mystical. The incarnational aspect of Christian faith is therefore most at risk with this model. There is also the danger of seeing your own form of church as the only or most legitimate, with the resultant loss of the sense of the wider church catholic. Finally, this form of church tends to neglect the organisational aspects of the church. The accountability and transparency of Church authority and governance is therefore at risk of compromise. As in the sociology of cults, charismatic people can assume leadership and power where governance structures have not been established. Thankfully most emerging churches have addressed the need for structure and models of leadership, but it remains a weakness of this model, and as such remains a work in progress. However, I have also met these very same problems in more traditional forms of church.

Sacramental Model of Church
The notion of Church as sacrament is Dulles' second model of church. In this typology, the church becomes an event of grace as the lives of its members are transformed in hope, joy, self-forgetful love, peace, patience, and in other Christ-like virtues.[16] A sacrament is a sign of God's grace, of God's gift. It is socially constituted, a communal symbol of grace coming to fulfilment. The main advantage of this second model is that sacrament becomes a visible sign of the presence of the revealed God, so that spectators may encounter God or, at least, recognise the significance of the Church as a numinous sign. For most Church traditions, the climax of sacrament is expressed in Holy Communion or Eucharist, with people gathered around to eat the bread and drink the wine. The church becomes a local expression of the gathering of all people, brought together through the presence of God, as Christ commanded at the last supper. God's mystical transcendent presence made immanent. The implications for mission are profound,

---

[15] Dulles, *Models* 44-53.
[16] Dulles, *Models* 55-63.

when God is understood as being made present by the activity and presence of Christians in our local communities. It is clear that some Emerging Church have made this connection:

> *A gift of the emerging church is that we see God equally in the Eucharist and in drinking beer together in the local bar.*[17]

> *Emerging churches tend to have rediscovered a more sacramental approach to everyday life...we gather around weekly Eucharist...We try to take a sacramental view of the whole of creation...A sacramental life is a life lived in God, so each day is sacramental and we ourselves are sacraments of God in the world...A defining characteristic of church has to be the regular participation in the community in Eucharist.*[18]

You may notice that this last quote makes connections between the sacramental and panentheism. This is no coincidence because there is a real connection between the idea of God's blessing through his presence in the bread and wine and in the sustaining power of the Spirit in nature. When the sacraments are understood in combination with perichoresis, kenosis and panentheism, the relationship between God, the Church and world becomes an expression of God's presence in, and commitment to the world. This understanding is somewhat neglected in the Western church. The church is instituted and constituted by the Trinity, and commissioned to acts of worship, mission and community in loving service to God in the world. By drawing on these two models of Church we have an authentic expression of church, the deep theological meaning of which resonates with the vision and values of the emerging Church.

Ekklesia and Transformative Community
The concept of the 'body of Christ' as used by the Apostle Paul connects with his use of the concept 'Ekklesia', a New Testament word meaning Church, or literally a 'gathering or assembly of people'.[19] It is also understood to reflect the idea of an alternative community, one which seeks to embody the values of the 'now but not yet' Kingdom of

---

[17] Mobsby, *Emerging & Fresh*, 60.
[18] Mobsby, *Emerging & Fresh*, 59.
[19] P Ward, *Liquid Church*, (Carlisle: Pater Noster Press, 2002) 6-9, B A Harvey, *Another City*, (Harrisburg: Trinity Press International, 1999), 150.

God.[20] It is a community that does not seek to remove itself from the world, but to transform it as Christ did through his ministry and the ministry of the disciples.[21]

> *[The Church] as the new social organism, springing from the words of Jesus in calling the twelve, with a citizen body which scandalously included from the beginning slaves, women and even children, persons, who had no place in the traditional ecclesia...obeyed his [Jesus'] new commandment to love irrespective of blood ties or social class.*[22]

The original 'ekklesia', from which the early Church derived its meaning, was an alternative to the town council or local legislator in the Greek speaking parts of the Roman Empire,[23] and was ruled by the wealthy male elite. The Church sought to be an alternative ekklesia, and therefore it included the powerless, such as slaves, the poor and women within its ranks.[24] It sought to live out the Kingdom in the 'now but not yet', on social, economic and political levels, including the spiritual.[25] As a consequence, those once excluded from society were 're-membered', or included in the Church.[26]

> *Christianity entered history as a new social order...From the very beginning Christianity was not primarily a "doctrine", but...a "community"...a New Community, distinct and peculiar...to which members were called and recruited...Primitive Christians felt themselves to be closely knit together...in a unity which radically transcended all*

---

[20] Grenz, *Ecclesiology*, 257-60.
[21] Harvey, *Another*, 15-6, 25.
[22] RCW Chartres, Ecclesiology – Edmonton Area Conference 15-vi-2004, as retrieved 7.01.2006 from the World Wide Web,
'http://www.klisia.net/blog/BishopoflondonaddressEcclesiology-EdmontonAreaConference.15-vi-2004.pdf', 2-3.
[23] P Avis, *The Anglican Understanding of Church*, (London: SPCK, 2000),1. Harvey, another, 23.
[24] Charters, *Ecclesiology*, 2-3. M Maggay Transforming Society, (Oxford: Lynx, 1994), 31-3, 36-7, 49-50.
[25] Harvey, *Another,* 17-22. Ward, liquid, 9-10.
[26] Charters, *Ecclesiology*, 3. Harvey, another, 57. Maggay, transforming, 15.

> *human boundaries – of race, of culture, of social rank, and indeed the whole dimension of "this world".*[27]

This concept of 're-membering' also makes connection with the sacramental understanding of the significance of the Ekklesia: that at the Last Supper, Jesus re-membered the new Ekklesia through the inauguration of the Eucharist or Holy Communion. To re-member symbolises our coming together, and in so doing, our living out what Christ called us to be. Christ becomes alive to the world through us. Christ becomes present as we retell and live the narrative of God.

> *The re-membering that Jesus commanded us to undertake was more profound than simply remembering past events. We are called to nothing less than a re-membering of Christ's body on earth having understood that everything in heaven and on earth should find their head and centre in the Word made flesh. In this way we are called into participation...in the round dance of the Trinity, the perichoresis.*[28]

This original understanding of ekklesia has been lost because of the process of institutionalisation that has since occurred. However, it is this authors contention that, whether consciously or not, the emerging church rediscovered something of this understanding through the use of Rublev's ikon. It is a model of church that draws on the strength of the mystical communion and sacramental models of church, with a focus on being an alternative inclusive church community drawing on a reading of ekklesia. The Emerging Church has come a long way!

The Wisdom of Richard Hooker
The Reformation in Britain is marked out as one of the more painful periods in church history. The expectation of 'unity in conformity' throughout the Tudor period, swung violently between Catholic and Protestant interpretations of what the true church was. In this conformity model, Christians were literally killing each other. Some theologians appreciated the need for a more diverse church, and sought an ecclesiology that somehow held both traditions in tension. Richard Hooker, an Anglican Divine was one of these.[29] His writings drew on

---

[27] G florovsky in Harvey, *Another*, 21-2.
[28] Charters, *Ecclesiology*, 3.
[29] I go into a lot of detail here in my first book, Mobsby, *Emerging*, 69-72.

both the mystical communion model and the sacramental model of Church, to try to hold Catholic and Protestant together. He also drew on the perichoretic nature of God, adopting the trinitarian model of community as 'unity in diversity', with a broad centre.[30] In *The Laws of Ecclesiastical Polity,* Hooker's trinitarian ecclesiology attempts to hold both Protestant and Catholic in tension, and yet also exclude fundamentalist expressions at either extreme. So why is this important? Well firstly, it is saying that an understanding of the Trinity has helped the Church to deal with difference and unity. This 'both and' approach is therefore not new. Some Emerging and Fresh Expressions of Church are rediscovering resources that have a tradition within some of our historic denominations.

Fraternity as New Monasticism
A mixture of emerging Churches, Fresh Expressions of Church and mission initiatives arising out of the charismatic traditions, have begun describing themselves as new monastic communities. They again draw on a combination of the Mystical Communion Model and Sacramental Model, with a core concern to engage with the question of how we should live. The most successful of these have experimented with a combination of church centred on place and network, with intentional communities, cafes and centres to practice hospitality. Many also have a rhythm, or rule of life to express what it means to be a Christian in a postmodern context.

The original Christian monastic orders, such as the Benedictines and the Franciscans, modelled how to be 'both and' communities, by drawing on a mystical communion model of church. Both in their time were fresh forms of church, which sought simultaneously to be radical new communities practising companionship and hospitality, and as participating, accountable members of the wider mother church. Both religious orders expressed a fraternal approach to church as a reaction to the increasingly institutional church they were accountable to at the time. They practiced the radical counter-values of powerlessness and poverty. In this way they attempted to be alternative radical communities to the church they were part of, whilst relating missionally to the contemporary culture of their times. This was a culture of mysticism, superstition and the spiritual, and their spirituality was an attempt to recontextualise the faith in an intelligible way. In a similar way, new

---

[30] *Ibid.*

Monastic communities are attempting to relate to a culture of mysticism in a twenty-first century context, modelling expressions of the Christian faith that can relate to this culture. We will explore this culture of new-mysticism more explicitly in the next chapter.

For the purpose of this book, I want to draw on what has been learnt from the emerging forms of 'new monasticism': specifically, Church of the Apostles in Seattle, USA, mayBE and hOME in Oxford, and the project in London with which I am personally involved, 'Moot'.

Flat Leadership & collaborative decision-making
One important structural value of both old and new monastic communities is the sense of fraternity or collegiality. Traditionally, would-be members join the local *Chapter* and make a full, annual commitment to a rule or rhythm of life; new monastic communities have also taken up this practice. The Chapter is given support and guidance by elected Priors, and the Abbot or Abbess, who also chair administrative matters. Some have different levels of belonging, so that a spiritual path from the third to first order of belonging can be followed. In both old and new forms there is a strong sense of shared decision-making and leadership, so that roles and responsibilities are exercised by all. Such roles are performed as a matter of function, not of power or privilege. This interpretation of a mystical communion model corrects a weakness regarding visible governance structures, and therefore some emerging churches have adopted it. Some, like Moot, have opted instead to adopt a rhythm of life as an aspirational statement, to which all are encouraged to commit at an annual service before the Bishop of London on Holy Saturday, during Easter week. Such forms of Church clearly reflect a perichoretic understanding of church.

Rhythm of Life
Many of the emerging new monastic communities have reinterpreted the ancient form of a rule or rhythm of life. They seek to answer the question 'How should we live?' rather that 'What should we believe?' This is a particularly important approach because it expresses what the Christian faith means in practice, encapsulating the values of discipleship, social, economic and ecological justice, balance and spirituality, all in the context of a mystical communion and sacramental

model. To demonstrate this, I will list the Moot community's Rhythm of Life, created in 2007.[31]

> *We live the moot rhythm of life through presence, acceptance, creativity, balance, accountability and hospitality*
>
> *presence*
> *We commit to journeying together with God and each other, by meeting together as a community, in prayer in worship, friendship, grief, and happiness. Being a hopeful sign of an open community in the city rather than just a group of individuals or anonymous people.*
>
> *acceptance*
> *We desire to accept both ourselves and other people as they are, and to allow people to say what they believe without fear of judgment. We want to create a safe space where people feel at home and welcomed. We hope to learn from all those in and outside the*
> *Community.*
>
> *creativity*
> *We want to have an open approach to how we learn, live and encounter God in the plurality of our city and the world. We wish to be creative in our worship, in prayer, in our lives, in learning, and with the Christian tradition, in our theology and with the arts.*
>
> *balance*
> *We aspire to live with integrity in the city, striving as a community for balance between work, rest and play. We wish to develop healthy spiritual disciplines such as daily prayer, meditation and contemplation, drawing on the ancient Christian paths. We want to live within our means, living sustainable lives. We desire to not be simply consumers, but people committed to giving and receiving in all of life.*

---

[31] As retrieved 7.01.2007 from the World Wide Web, 'http://www.mootblog.net'.

accountability
Within the rhythm of life we desire to be accountable to one another, to grow and journey together, listening to each other and the wider Christian community for wisdom rather than trusting only ourselves. We want to have a willingness to share life, rather than to privatise it and we seek to walk together in a deep way rather than as strangers who only know the surface of each other.

hospitality
We wish to welcome all whom we encounter, when we are gathered and when we are dispersed, extending Christ's gracious invitation to relationship, meaning and life in all its fullness.

This Rhythm of Life is an innovative way of expressing the Christian faith in the context of contemporary culture. Some have expressed their concern that such rhythms of life are not explicit concerning the nature of God or the more traditional Christian confessional message. But this is surely missing the point. As people encounter Christians living out profound expressions of the faith through God's love, they encounter the depth of a loving Christian community and experience God as their 'Ground of being', through worship, mission and community. Such an approach explicitly trusts the Holy Spirit to bring meaning and spiritual experience to people as they encounter Christians living out their faith in the ordinariness of life. It is in these participative and loving Christian communities that people can encounter the reality of the Christian story of the Holy Trinity, not as hypothetical truth, but as a profound reality, clueing us in as to how we should live.

Participation in doing
The key value of these forms of church is that they are totally dependent on the involvement and shared leadership of the people of God. People are not merely involved, but actually lead the various activities, and thereby help to fully express the dynamic of a spiritual community. This understanding of church as a participative spiritual event reflects the Trinitarian understanding of God as an event. This keeps the church healthy, as such forms of church are only as good as the relationships of which they consist. This is lost in forms of church that require people to be passive, or to leave their personalities or brains

at the door of the church. People learn about God more through spiritual experience and encounter, than by the acquisition facts.

Mission consideration
This approach to being Church is fully open to the postmodern pursuit of learning through experience. Purely learning facts about God is an inadequate approach in contemporary culture. Traditional forms of church usually hold to the pattern that says that belief is a necessary prerequisite for belonging. In a postmodern context this effectively excludes many people. If people need spiritual experiences to work out what, and if they believe, then an approach that enables people to belong to such communities as unbelievers is crucial if we are to be committed to appropriate forms of mission and evangelism. This 'belonging without believing' is a core value of emerging church communities, and it is made increasingly possible through the use of rhythms or rules of life. Such an approach trusts in the inspiration of the Holy Spirit beckoning and revealing the nature of God to those who are not yet Christian. In this way God, through new forms of church, draws people into restored relationship with the divine, helping them shift from spiritual tourism to Christian pilgrimage.

Reflection: Why are these models of church important?
In our postmodern context, there is a desperate need for models of church that are able to function and relate to contemporary culture, and which express the truths of Christianity through loving service. Whether we like it or not, some current forms of church, and the faith they express, are anachronistic and do not help people encounter the deep love of God in a positive, health-giving form.

What I cannot understand is how some forms of church express so much hatred, hardness and elitism, making the love of God seem such a long way off. Much preaching appears to appeal to the power of guilt and shame rather than loving inspiration. I am sure that this is due in part to fundamentalist expressions of faith, where everything must be kept simple, and black and white. We must resist simplistic solutions in our expression of church, and embrace the necessary complexity of living out our faith in a complex world. A dear friend, who was told a lie in the name of the supposedly loving Christian God, helped bring this home to me most vividly. After years of trying to make a failing marriage work, through counselling, marriage guidance and prayer ministry, he reached the point where there was nowhere else to go. Having decided, after much heartache, to get a divorce, he sought out the Pastor of a local church for guidance. He was told that what he was about to do was wrong, and that the church did not have a duty to support Christians seeking divorce. He was further informed that he was removing himself from the love of God, and from the Church by his actions. He was effectively excluded from Church and from God (as he understood it) because he was seeking pragmatic solutions to the very real problems of his life. My friend came to me in the middle of the night and in deep pain and tears to ask, *"Will God ever love me again?"*

I can't express how angry this made me then, and now as I recollect it. I told him through my own tears, that God had never stopped loving him, and that there was no such thing as the doctrine of limited grace. This false teaching justifies the thinking of fundamentalist Christians and has effectively wrecked the spiritual and social lives of many people. The research I conducted for my previous book has convinced me that this approach to the Christian faith has successfully de-churched a great many people. The shame it creates often causes people to walk away from God, and to limit the power of the infinite love of God. No human being has the right to define who is in and who is out, when the love of God is concerned. Such beliefs must be challenged by those prepared to model alternative expressions of Christian community.

I believe that the large number of controlling leaders in the Church is a reflection of particular models of church. Too much unaccountable power in the hands of an individual in a hierarchical context often results in the institutionalisation not only the church community, but also its leader. Power always distorts, its part of the darker side of our human nature. Christendom, a model of church with centralised and hierarchical power structures, was created in a time of royalty and nobility. Such a model appears to me to be utterly anachronistic, a wholly inaccurate reflection of the idea of ekklesia - an alternative inclusive and participative community.

The models of church we have looked at seek to draw on the perichoretic nature of the Holy Trinity, as an alternative to some of the more aggressive forms of church. I do believe that God has led the emerging Church in this way, so as to counter the increasingly hard-line, loveless forms of fundamentalist churches increasingly found today. Increasingly these churches model a 'church as business' approach, which overtime becomes hierarchical and oppressive, with the church leaders gaining enormous power. In so doing, they become the new Pharisees and Sadducees. There is a need to return to the values and forms of Church modelled in the New Testament. It will be exciting to review what has happened in another ten years.

Church needs to relate to the culture in which it finds itself, and we increasingly live in world driven by information technology, consumption and postmodern sensibilities. How does a Church drawing on the relational and transcendent aspects of the Holy Trinity operate in such a world? We will explore this in the next chapter.

Chapter Five

Ancient:Future Church in the 21st-Century of the hyper-real

It was a warm spring day, and I was in the Royal Horticultural Hall in central London at the annual Mind Body and Spirit Festival. The hall was divided up into over one hundred and fifty exhibition units. The festival took the form of a trade show of everything you could think of in the name of inner peace and spirituality. Amongst the massage healers, crystals, auragram machinery and feng shui book sellers, was the Dekhomai stall. Dekhomai, the Greek for 'the welcoming place', was the name given to a cooperative of a number of London based Christians, which included members of Moot, some CMS employees, a few local Anglo-Catholic Christians, and a charismatic house church. Some Christians think that these festivals are for a fringe minority, and while this was the case in the 1960s and 1970s, it no longer holds in the 21st century. There is currently a renewed interest in all things spiritual rather than traditional forms of religion. Two thousand people visited the festival each of the four days it was open, which is at least 8000 people, each paying over £20 just to get it in: spirituality is no longer a minority sport. For the small fee of £20, one could bang a gong for fifteen minutes and discover inner centeredness; a variety of crystals were on sale (at anything from £20 to £2000) to help channel your energy so you could sleep at night; or you could have your tarot cards read for £30. In the midst of this spiritual market place, a bunch of Christians put together a stall offering free massage, anointing with oil, prayer, and direction in various forms of Christian meditation – 'Christian Spirituality to go', and for free. I massaged feet, and gave the occasional blessing, and just took the time to talk, and listen to whoever came along. It was an incredible privilege to love people, to listen to their stories, and to offer hope and prayer. Many were confused that our ministry was for free. Others couldn't work out how Christians, associated with Church, could be so loving: surely there was a catch? Most came with a keen sense of their own pain, and visited each stall in a desperate search for authenticity and spiritual relief. As I massaged, people would relax and begin to open up, sharing their deep struggles, passions, desire to belong, desire for love, desire to be more human and less busy. In the midst of all of this I prayed and blessed people in the name of the Creator, Redeemer and Companion. People laughed, people cried, people were still, and people appeared to experience profound things of God in that little place. My hope is that our diverse little bunch of Christians enabled people to encounter the Holy Trinity, and that God was able to pour out the divine love through us. It was precisely the place church should be, and in a form that made God accessible and authentic to the brave new world of mysticism in our culture.

Many in the Western Church have yet to realise, that rather than succumbing to increased secularisation and disbelief, spirituality has become an issue of exponentially greater significance in recent years. Unfortunately for the Church, this interest in things spiritual often excludes of traditional forms of religion.[1]

---

[1] There has been a lot of discussion about whether this is true following a research project that explored whether young people going to a nightclub made any associations with religious imagery or ideas. The research showed that young people have no residual appreciation for religious ideas. Those critical of the research indicate that the research asked the wrong questions – which should be orientated towards 'spirituality' rather than 'religion' and for which the sample size was quite small. For more information see http://easyasfallingoffablog.blogspot.com/2006/09/spirituality-of-generation-y.html.

The rise of holistic spirituality and techgnosis with the demise of religion

The Times published this bold headline in 2006: *"Christianity will be eclipsed by spirituality in 30 years, startling new research predicts. Our correspondent reports on the collapse of traditional religion and the rise of mysticism."*[2] Now, it is questionable whether thirty years is an accurate prediction for the demise of Christianity, but the rise of new mysticism as a form of spirituality is not. Lets clarify what we mean when we talk about spirituality in this way. Yvonne Richmond has in my view given the best definition:

> *'Spirituality' has become an 'in' word; today it covers everything from different moral and ethical codes in a diverse range of esoteric, sometimes occult practices. It is largely influenced by Eastern religions and the New Age Movement, with their emphasis on attaining higher consciousness in the search for the divine, the interrelatedness of all things, and holistic healing...people are looking for new solutions to the struggles they face. (Yvonne Richmond, 2007)*[3]

So rather than turning to atheism and secularization, our culture appears to be turning to a belief in mysticism. This is supported by research (Hay and Hunt, 2002) that looked at the changes in spiritual experiences or perceptions. The results are significant.[4]

Spiritual Experience/Perception	1987	2000	% Increase
A patterning of events/transcendent providence	29%	50%	90%
Awareness of the presence of God	27%	38%	41%

---

[2] C Midgley, *Spirited away: why the end is nigh for religion*, The Times Newspaper 4th November 2006. P Heelas, L Woodhead, B Seel, K Tusting, The Spiritual Revolution: Why Religion is Giving Way to Spirituality, (London: Blackwell, 2007).

[3] Y Richmond, N Spencer, S Croft, *Evangelism in a Spiritual Age: Communicating Faith in a Changing Culture*, (Church House Publishing, 2007), 8.

[4] Hay, Hunt *Frequency of report of religious or spiritual experience in Britain for years 1987 and 2000* in D Hay *'Experience'* in A Holder (ed.) *A Blackwell Companion to Christian Spirituality*, (Oxford: Blackwell, 2007), 417-441. Y Richmond et al, *Evangelism*, 11.

Awareness of prayer being answered	25%	37%	48%
Awareness of a sacred presence in nature	16%	29%	81%
Awareness of the presence of the dead	18%	25%	39%
Awareness of an evil presence	12%	25%	108%
CUMULATIVE TOTAL		48%	76%

These statistics show that something is changing in our extremely cynical postmodern world. The changes are however, emphatically not in the favour of traditional religion, as the results of other recent research bears out very clearly.[5] The vast majority of people in the UK have either given up on church or never had anything to do with it.[6] This leaves a residual twenty percent of people who regularly attend, where 'regularly attending' means one visit per month. Official statistics estimate that forty percent of the population is de-churched – meaning that they have either drifted away from church due to changes in work or home circumstances, because of a bad experience of church leadership, or because they could not make any sense of the gap between their lives in the real world, and the world of church. This leaves a further forty percent who were non-churched, who have never attended.[7] Remarkably however, many people consider themselves to be Christian, but would express this more in terms of spirituality:

> *In 2000, sixty percent of the population claimed to belong to a specific religion with fifty five percent being Christian. However, half of all adults aged eighteen and over who belonged to a religion have never attended a religious service.*[8]

We see here the rise of a 'pic 'n' mix', individualistic interpretation of religion, which is again more about spiritual tourism, spiritual fulfilment, and the quest for inner peace and wholeness.[9]

---

[5] Sources: BSA 2004, European Social Survey 2002, BgbF 1996/7, Tearfund 2005/6, ORB 2005, Populas 2006, HMSO 2000, Christian Research 2006.
[6] P Richer, *Gone but not forgotten,* (London: DLT, 1998) in Cray et al., *A Mission Shaped Church,* (London: CHP. 2004), 37-8.
[7] G Cray et al., *A Mission Shaped Church,* (London: CHP, 2004), 39. A Jamieson *A Churchless faith*, (London: SPCK), 9, 16.
[8] HMSO, *Belonging to Religion: Social Trends 32*, (London: HMSO, 2000).
[9] M. McCarthy, *Spirituality in a Post modern Era*, in J. Woodward, S. Pattison (eds.), *A Blackwell Reader in Pastoral and Practical Theology.* (Oxford: Blackwell Publishers, 2000), 193-6.

The point of tourist life is to be on the move, not to arrive...there is no goal beckoning at the end of life's travel's...impulse and spontaneity become the new control...[10]

This is not an easy journey for spiritually searching, or the traditionally religious among us. The sense of nihilism, disorientation, pain, insecurity and liminality is often acute. What we are facing is the change of a paradigm, a change in the very way we perceive reality. As Lyon states:

Traditional religious outlooks, with their fixed points, transcendent anchors, and universal scope, seem out of kilter with the emerging spirit of the age.[11]

In the pre-modern mind, (the time before the Enlightenment) reality consisted in the God or gods above, and the devil or beasts below. There was a strong sense of the sacred and of transcendence, which we see reflected in the imagery of creation in Genesis Chapter One. Spiritual experience and mysticism were an accepted part of everyday life. Modernist thinkers (from the Enlightenment until the mid-20th century) deliberately rejected transcendence and mysticism, seeing them as little more than 'hocus pocus' superstition. Knowledge was divided between object and subjective truth, where the subjective had no value. Emphasis was on objective fact; there was nothing more than the physical world, the observable here and now. During this time the mysticism of the pre-modern mindset didn't disappear, it just went underground (however both mindsets continued to operate within the Church). This has shifted again in the latter part of the twentieth century with the advent of postmodernity (this is also expressed *liquid modernity,* but more often by those who see the period of time in question as a continuation of modernity, and not the beginning of a new epoch). People realised that those who proclaimed the 'objective' as truth were not being fully honest, as all experience and truth is ultimately subjective. Therefore the central tenets of the scientific method are perceived to be increasingly limited. No longer objectively

---

[10] Z Bauman, *Postmodernity and its discontents*, (Cambridge: Polity Press, 1997), 90-4.

[11] D Lyon, *Jesus in Disneyland,* (Oxford: Polity Press, 2002), 14.

certain, knowledge is seen as provisional, contextual and subjective.[12] The new postmodern sensibility dictates the primacy of the subjective over the supposedly objective.

We live in a culture defined by consumption, pluralism, uncertainty, immediacy and individuality. This has become so pervasive that many people define themselves by the labels their wear, the cars they driver, and the bars they attend, creating a new 'pick' n' mix' lifestyle.[13] So for those who have money, consumption has become the new strategy for defining ones identity. Immediately we can see how this excludes the poor; many young people have therefore turned to geographic, turf tribalism as a response. The great sadness of our times is the loss of a sense of common humanity created by the culture of consumption. What happens when your partner dies, you loose your job, you get depressed? What does one do with such a life strategy? Many of us indulge in a little retail therapy. We reinvent or re-affirm ourselves through a seemingly limitless supply of credit. Life is lived in the eternal present, 'live for today as tomorrow may never come'. It is a consumptive life, based on the model of the eternal tourist who never arrives at their destination. So we travel light, trying to ensure that cumbersome commitments are kept to a minimum. As a solution, this doesn't go very deep, and when trouble hits, which inevitably it will our patterns of consumption become addictive. The following two examples will illustrate my point.

The first concerns the two key characters in the film *Fight Club*, who meet at a number of twelve-step support group for various addictions or health conditions. They start to tour a variety of different support groups with a view to encountering the real, raw emotion of suffering people, and the compassion, belonging and care shared between sufferers. They start regularly attending some of these support groups even though they do not suffer from any of the conditions or addictions the groups were set up for. The relief from stress that they experience helps them sleep at night.

The second example I would like to give, is the opening story in Adbusters Magazine. The inside front cover has a picture of a crying girl surrounded by bottles of alcohol and other consumer products.

---

[12] M P Gallagher, *Clashing Symbols An Introduction to Faith & Culture*, (London: DLT), 100-4. If you want more details, see my first book "Emerging & Fresh Expressions of Church".

[13] S Taylor, *The out-of-bounds church? Learning to create communities of faith in a culture of change*, (Grand Rapids, USA: Zondervan, 2005), 24-7, 88.
Z Bauman, *Liquid Modernity*, (Oxford: Polity Press, 2000), 1-14, 53-63, 92.

Above the picture is the title "The quest for an authentic life", and the following lines:

> *One glorious day, a girl sat down to write. Her mind was blank with only hazy thoughts. Her life was a joke, full of bullshit and filth. She was dirty in a dirty place. Who cares about her anyways? The room was empty, devoid of furniture or sign of life, besides the empty pizza boxes scattered around the room. Her life was trash, just like the room. Pain was her only true companion. Tears filled her eyes as she stared down at the blank paper. The coloured lines began to blur from the salty water. She sat still, wallowing in the depths of her infinite sorrow...Is this voice in the back of my mind fooling me? Am I really a unique human being with my own body, mind and soul, on my own magic journey of life? Or is this feeling of separateness an illusion, the source of all my anxiety and angst? Sometimes I'm afraid...I'll make a habit of presenting to be other people. There's the charm of the twenty-first century living, isn't it? Let's play make-believe! I'll make up life stories for entirely fictional characters, with fictional friends and fictional accents and fictional personalities.*[14]

Both of these examples illustrate the point that, despite the illusion presented, consumption does not bring lasting spiritual relief. Instead it increases ones stress and the sense of liminality. And most importantly, it doesn't help answer the existential questions of Who am I?, Where do I belong?, and What am I? These unanswered questions drive people into a quest for meaning and belonging, often as spiritual tourists at events like the Mind, Body and Spirit Festivals. The equally powerful and influential force of information technology also helps to drive this consumptive spiritual questing.

For those who can remember, think about what your life was like before fax machines, before laptops, email, mobile phones, the Internet, and text messaging. Information technology has transformed our lives into a constant flow of information; often all we can is try to keep our heads above water.[15] We now live in a global village of immediate communication. The world of information technology has

---

[14] A Gill, *The quest for an authentic life*, Adbusters Journal of the Mental Environment, Volume 15 Number 4, July/August 2007.

[15] Lyon, *Disneyland*, 13-4, 37. Caputo *On*, 67-8, 76-7.

also opened us to the concept of cyber, or virtual reality. This means that the modernist concept of reality, as all about the objective, the here and now of a purely physical world, no longer applies. There is a new sense of otherness and transcendence in the popular psyche, and it is mediated by information technology. Surprisingly, our highly technical postmodern culture has given life, once again, to something of a pre-modern mindset.

Rollins, Caputo and Davis all attribute the renewed interest in spirituality directly to the reality of a new form of transcendence and spirituality, a new spiritual belief in the impossible:

> *The impossible has recently become possible again, that the very force of modernist criticism when turned on itself opens the way for a post-critical and post-secular posture that accommodates the passion for the impossible. That movement of living on the limit of the possible, in hopeful expectation of the impossible, a reality beyond the real, which I take to be the mark of a religious sensibility...We live...in a world of high-tech advanced telecommunication systems, a dizzying world that is changing everything...Religion shows every sign of flourishing in a new high-tech form.*[16]

> *Cell phones whose signals easily penetrate thick walls, satellites that link across the globe...we have found a way to mime the angels.*[17]

> *We are faced with an amazing – shall we say an impossible? – situation: the simultaneous flourishing of science and religion*[18]*, and indeed, at its extremes, of advanced hardball science along with some far out screwball superstition. We live in a world where the most sophisticated scientific and high tech achievements cohabit...Fundamentalists New-Age spiritualities and belief in all sorts of bizarre hocus-pocus phenomena...However there is increasing rejection of traditional forms of spirituality.*[19]

---

[16] Caputo, *On*, 67-8.
[17] Caputo, *On*, 70.
[18] I would argue that he meant 'spirituality' but I am being faithful to the quote.
[19] Caputo, *On*, 70.

So this hyper-real[20] form of spirituality, the seeking of the impossible over the real, makes connections with pre-modern forms of mysticism, reframing them for a new postmodern context:

> *So here we are: a hyper-technological and cynically postmodern culture seemingly drawn like a passel of moths toward the glittering flames of the pre-modern mind.*[21]

> *Today's techgnotics find themselves, consciously or not, surrounded by a complex set of ideas, and images: transcendence through technology...*[22]

In seeking answers to life's key questions, we find ourselves in a culture gripped by the search for transcendence and new (or rather I should say old) forms of mysticism. This is not a new situation; much of the pre-modern world was on the same quest. In fact, before the invention of the printing press, the Catholic Church constructed a form of liturgy that utilised all the senses, so as to engage with a world that was centred on mysticism. It is therefore unsurprising that alternative worship groups have often reframed ancient liturgies, and resources like the Labyrinth, for use with a postmodern audience. The approach used is therefore often described as *ancient:future*.

The model used by Monks and Friars in the pre-modern era, characterised by radical inclusion and hospitality for spiritual tourists, has been a key source of inspiration for the new monastic movements of postmodern times. It is no coincidence that the British reality TV shows 'The Monastery' and 'The Convent' were hugely popular (these programs charted the experience of a small group people spending an extended period of time with a monastic community). This new, hyper-real spirituality undoubtedly presents something of an opportunity for the Church, but most likely not in its traditional form. The Church has a calling to help those who find themselves in the context of new mysticism, to shift from the endless path of the eternal spiritual tourist, to the purposeful journey of a Christian pilgrim.

---

[20] P J Rollins, *His Colour is our Blood: A phenomenology of the prodigal Father PhD thesis* (Belfast: Queen's University, 2004), 117-20. E Davis, *TechGnosis, Myth, Magic and Mysticism in the Age of Information*, (London: Serpents Tail, 2004), 4-10.

[21] Davis, *Techgnosis*, 5.

[22] Davis, *Techgnosis*, 122.

Unsettling of the Spirit?
As Pete Rollins reminds us, the postmodern turn to the subject has helped us see that our very lives allow us to experience the Christian God as radically subjective. God's immanence is hyper-present, so that we encounter the divine though the subjective experience of the presence of God in the ordinariness of our lives.[23] I would argue that this yearning for transcendence is the continuing work of the Sustainer and Perfecter, the Spirit of God. I would pose the question: Might virtual reality conceivably provide for the possibility of an 'I-thou' encounter? Have the vehicles of information technology and consumption, imperfect and flawed pursuits of humanity though they are, become an opportunity for transformative encounter with the Holy Spirit? I believe this to be the case.

The Moot Community website now receives fifteen thousand hits per month, and most of these are from spiritual tourists.[24] There are at least two or three new people at each service who claim to have discovered us through the Internet. This is the case for many alternative worship and emerging Church communities. And when you consider the number of services happening every month, that's a lot of people. Therefore, I would like to argue, unlike some writers, such as Michael Frost,[25] that God is still present in the incompleteness and brokenness of the post-industrial, consumerist Western culture. What is absolutely not needed, is a withdrawal from the world for fear of it being Godless. The great danger of seeing oneself as separate from the world, as a stranger in a foreign country, is that it predisposes us to the 'sin of Holiness' that Riddell has warned us of. We develop at mindset that says, 'we are right and they are wrong'; this creates an attitude of superiority and certainty, which often leads to fundamentalism. The Church must never loose its trust in a God who is present in all of creation and in all cultures. When it does, it experiences distortion in its ministry. As Harvey stated:

> *Christian communities must learn to deal with the problems and possibilities posed by life in the "outside" world. But of more importance, any attempt on the part of the church to*

---

[23] Rollins, *How (Not)*, 23-4. Rollins, *His Colour, 4-10*.

[24] These numbers are measured by online tracking software. This software also enables analysis of what subjects people were searching for. This data suggests the search for forms of spirituality relevant for spiritual searchers.

[25] M Frost, *Exiles, Living Missionally in a Post-Christian Culture,* (Peabody: Hendrickson Publishers, 2006), 81-104.

withdraw from the world would be in effect a denial of its mission.[26]

Such a withdrawal would undermine the 'both and' balancing act of holding incarnational and redemptive theologies in tension. Such a retreat into the over emphasis of redemptive theology would be to repeat the historical mistakes of the Western Church. The challenge for Church is how to be in but not of contemporary culture.

I may be an overly optimistic, romantically minded Christian, but I believe it is possible to maintain such radical, theological tension; I also believe that our world, which seems increasingly violent and dehumanising, needs it now more than ever. My own incompleteness compels me to hold onto the hope that the Trinitarian God is as involved in the world of the 21st century, as much as any other. I believe that the Universe is still inherently good and beautiful, and that humanity is still being beckoned into relationship with the divine. Rather than spelling the end of religion, the concept of techgnosis gives me even greater faith in God's presence, and it encourages my belief in the impossible. After all, it was foundational for my own conversion to Christianity from a long line of atheists. There are however some downfalls to the new context of techgnosis.

The Danger of the pic 'n' mix God
At my lowest times, I fear that my ministry provides nothing more than a good exit strategy for falling out of relationship with the Christian God. I worry that I give permission for people to pic 'n' mix a God of their choosing, watering the traditional doctrines down so they fit obligingly with the individuals own pre-established values. In our current cultural climate, these are both very real threats. My greatest challenge is relating with those who define God by a set of consciously thought through consumptive processes, which tend to be self-centred, rather than mediated, or led by God. It is much easier, for example, to believe in a pluralist god, so that all religions are equally valid routes to the same God. The inconsistencies and differences of approach in the different religions are smoothed over, creating a personalised 'my-spirituality', dumbed-down, more palatable spirituality for the discerning postmodern, post-Christian consumer. That this approach undermines the Trinity and much of the narrative of the New Testament is a compromise that modern people should be able to bear. Now don't

---

[26] Harvey, *Another City*, 14.

hear me wrong, I do believe that there are truths in all religions and faiths, but I do believe that Christianity has the most distinctive yet imperfect understanding of the Holy Trinity. It is this distinctly Christian narrative that renders the concepts of salvation, perichoresis and the rest as possible. While I do think that God can use other religions to convey the Trinity, Christianity in my view, retains the best imperfect understanding amongst other imperfect understandings.

Many spiritual searchers do wrestle healthily with God on an existential level. However, the danger is one of not really seeking God for understanding. As a culture we are terrible at listening to one another because our skill-sets are centred on consumption. Instead of attending to the other, the human ego retains the power to define God without any attempt to seek. Only by attending to the mystical otherness of God in humility, powerlessness, and contemplative and creative prayer, can I develop an adequate subjective comprehension of who this God is. It has always seemed paradoxical to me that often those who are wrestling with God, do not believe in prayer, or any subjective spiritual experience other than 'conceptual thinking'. Their experience of God is almost entirely logical and of the mind, and mediated by the rigorous practice of certainty in their uncertainty. A high level of cynicism protects this position from of any of the more positive outlooks on offer.

For some, this is a phase of deconstruction, a healthy part of the process of finding a faith of their own. God often leads us into desert experiences, so that we can reconstruct a more mature and God led faith. The pattern of faith and doubt is a healthy expression of Christian discipleship. In fact, the Christian life can be a helix of ever continuing circles of orientation, disorientation and reorientation. Put another way, it can be seen as a cycle of life, death and resurrection, eventually being led by God into a more mature faith. But healthy deconstruction does require deeper engagement through to reconstruction. However some get stuck in deconstruction, and remain arm wrestling with God indefinitely. Only by finding what Paul Ricoeur calls a second naiveté and Dave Tomlinson's calls a second innocence, an ability to get beyond our doubts and thoughts, emotions and feelings, can you hear God for what God says. Only by letting go, and by acknowledging your need for God, will you allow God in. Douglas Coupland's book, *Life After God* is the epitome of this.

1000 years (*Life After God*), one of the short stories in the book, has the main protagonist, Scout, reach the climax of his spiritual quest in the symbolic setting of a forest. He is so unhappy with his experience of the contemporary postmodern world, that he has failed to return to work and is at his wits end. He clearly is expecting something extremely significant to occur, and is open about the possibility of some sort of spiritual encounter. He spends the night in his tent, which is pitched in a very remote spot, near a pool by a waterfall, and he now awaits the dawn:

> *Here I now lie, on my stomach, looking out at the dark wet world, pulling the blanket tighter around me, smoking a cigarette, and knowing that this is the end of some aspect of my life, but also the beginning – the beginning of some unknown secret that will reveal itself to me soon. All I need to do is pray... I kneel down and sip water from the pool. I raise my head and look through the clearing of the trees. I see the sun shining in the sky – a spinning ball of fire ... This same sun – the same burning orb of flame that shone over my youth – over...swimming pools and Lego and Kraft dinners and malls and suburbia and TV and books about Andy Warhol...I remove my blanket and fold it on the warm rocks beside the water. I then remove my shoes and socks and stick my feet into the water, and oh, it is cold...And the water from the stream above me roars. Oh does it roar! Like a voice that knows only one message, one truth – never-ending, like the clapping of hands and the cheers of the citizens upon the coronation of the king, the crowds of the inauguration, cheering for hope and for that one voice that will speak to them. Now here is my secret: I tell it to you with an openness of heart that I doubt I shall ever achieve again, so I pray that you are in a quiet room as you hear these words. My secret is that I need God – that I am sick and can no longer make it alone. I need God to help me give, because I no longer seem capable of giving; to help me be kind, as I no longer seem capable of kindness; to help me love, as I seem beyond being able to love. I walk deeper and deeper into the rushing water...the water enters my belly button and it freezes my chest, my arms, my neck. It reaches my mouth, my nose, my ears and the roar is so loud – this roar, this clapping hands. These hands – the hands that heal; the hands that hold, the hands we desire because they are better than desire. I submerge myself in the pool completely. I grab my knees and I forget gravity and I float within the pool and yet, even here, I hear the roar of water, the roar of clapping hands. These hands, the hands that care, the hands that mould; the hands that touch the lips, the lips that*

speak the words – the words that tell us we are whole.[27]

This kind of surrender is key in moving from a simplistic, unsustainable faith, to something more complex, open ended and sustainable. We need to constantly 'die to ourselves' in order be constantly 'born-again' in our walk with God. This is the walk of authentic Christian discipleship. If our life strategy remains purely consumptive, then we will not experience the incredible depths of God. It is by its nature a risky and uncertain journey, requiring us to let go of control. However it can in equal measure, be utterly resourcing and transformative.

Fundamentalism as the Impossible Faith of Techgnosis
This form of 'impossible', mystical spirituality is not all good news. The process of globalisation itself can create forms of postmodern fundamentalism. Belief in the 'impossible' can also create in Caputo's words an 'impossible people'. Fundamentalist forms of faith, oppressive, controlling and violent, can easily take root in our current spiritual environment.[28] Violence and oppression is so often the dark side of human passion. A strategy for dealing with the complexity of the world that is simplistic and 'black and white', will always require some degree of dehumanisation to maintain it. The challenge for progressive Christians is to live out a faith that is characterised by the values of love, powerlessness, non-violence, inclusion, generosity and hospitality, in the belief that God works through these, albeit at great personal cost to us.

Reflection
Personally I do believe that God, through the person of the Holy Spirit, is beckoning us through the joint effects of consumerism and techgnosis. There is a real danger that spiritual tourists and Christian Pilgrims become caught up projective thinking and neo-modernist forms of certainty, which become more important than discerning experience. But having said that, our times offer a real opportunity to those forms of church reflecting a mystical communion and sacramental model, and having an Ancient:Future approach to Church.

---

[27] D Coupland, *Life After God*, (London: Touchstone Books, 1994), 355-60.
[28] Caputo, *On*, 92-3, 108.

Chapter Six

Orthopraxis & Sacramentality reframed for the 21st-Century

At a recent Convention of emerging Churches there was a discussion about Sacraments and Church:

The emerging church is not shy about raiding the storehouses of the Roman Catholics, the Orthodox and the Anglicans for richer liturgies as well as prayer beads, icons, spiritual direction, lectio divina and a deeper sacramentality. The return to this ancient faith and practice is increasingly seen as a way forward in churches polarized by worship wars and theological intransigence. Thus, emerging churches often characterize themselves as "ancient-future," a phrase that comes from a series of books authored by Webber (Ancient-Future Faith, Ancient-Future Evangelism, Ancient-Future Time). This return to the past should not be confused with nostalgia for 1950s Protestantism or with a circling of the wagons around a purer Reformation theology. The return is deeper, looking to the

> *treasures of the medieval and patristic theologies and to practices that have long been ignored by evangelicals.*[1]

This ancient:future approach is part of an attempt to understand what it means to be Christian, drawing on the ancient to inform the current. This is not as easy as it sounds, and touches on what is called contextual theology, a much-maligned discipline by those of a conservative orientation. The task is difficult because you just can't take writings from the Cappadocian Fathers about the Trinity, or scriptural texts, and plonk them into postmodern cultures, and expect them to be understood and appreciated in their fullness. Worldviews, language, values and perceptions of the world today are totally different from those common in ancient times. So how and what the church does with these ancient writings and practices requires careful consideration. Contextual theology takes culture and cultural change seriously and attempts to understand the Christian faith in context,[2] where the language of biblical theology often does not resonate with contemporary experience. It has been defined as:

> *A way of doing theology in which one takes into account: the spirit and message of the gospel; the tradition of the Christian people; the culture in which one is theologising; and social change in that culture.*[3]

Barbour and Bevans propose that the various models of contextual theology attempt to create a symbolic system or framework to enable theologizing in context.[4] Models are understood to be logical theological positions that allow for some insights and connections. Each model differs in the balance they achieve between incarnational and redemptive theologies. Bevans proposes that there is a continuum between purely redemptive and purely incarnational focused models, and most models strike something of a balance between these two theologies.[5]

---

[1] S Bader-Saye, *A New Kind of Church, The Christian Century*, November 30, 2004, pp. 20-27.
[2] S B Bevans, *Models of contextual theology*, (New York: Orbis, 2002), 1-2, 5,7.
[3] Ibid, 1.
[4] Barber as recorded in Bevans, *Models*, 24-5.
[5] Bevans, *Models,* 24-5.

Part of the argument in my first book was that emerging and Fresh Expressions of church appear to be utilising a synthetic model of contextual theology for a distinctly postmodern context.[6] This model attempts to listen to culture for basic patterns and structures, and thereby pinpoint the basic symbol systems in operation. Out of such a "thick description" (holding many things in tension – scripture, culture and tradition) will *emerge* basic themes for the local theology. At the same time, however, these themes need to be in dialogue with the basic themes in gospel and tradition. This strategy, which holds on to the sense of an ancient:future faith, has a mutually transforming effect.[7] This particular relationship between Church and Culture relates to Niebuhr's synthetic approach, where 'Christ is above culture' but enters into it, and where culture is seen positively, as a vehicle for leading people to Christ.[8] Thinking about this again, I am left with a couple of questions. Where is the place for the 'I-Thou' relationship to bring transformative and subjective meaning out of the perichoretic nature of the Trinity? Where is the place for the meeting of the human imagination and the guidance of the Holy Spirit? These are not explicit in the Synthetic Model of contextual theology, but are very much present in another of Bevans' models, the Transcendent Model of contextual theology. I am therefore challenged to consider whether Trinitarian theology and an ecclesiology which is centred on perichoresis, kenosis and panentheism, requires the use of a more transcendent contextual theological perspective.

Bevans considers the transcendent model to be more focused on incarnational theology, (social change and culture), but influenced by redemptive theology, (gospel message and tradition) as a starting place.[9] The model assumes that the development of a truly contextualized theology takes place as an individual or people wrestle with their own faith and share that faith with others within the same cultural parameters. It assumes a process of questing and questioning for 'what is'.[10] It starts with one's own religious experience and experience of oneself. Exploration and encounter with God helps to articulate 'who I am' and 'who God is', as a product of subjective experience tied into a particular historical, geographical, social and

---

[6] Mobsby, *Emerging & Fresh*, 28-30.
[7] Bevans, *Models*, 86.
[8] Niebuhr, *Christ and culture*, in Percy, *The Salt of the Earth: Religious resilience in a Secular Age*, (London: Continuum, 2002), 36-40.
[9] Bevans, *Models*, 26-9.
[10] Bevans, *Models*, 97-104.

cultural context. God's revelation is transcendent but revealed in human experience. For this to work, such models assume that humankind operates in identical ways in all cultures and in all periods of history, and that the self-transcending subject possesses effective and cognitive operations. Revelation then relates to a change of mind, or thinking, literally a conversion from experience leading to a radical shift in perspective. This resonates with the phrase I have used repeatedly in this book: of 're-imagining another way'. Such a contextual theology 'will not appear primarily in books, but in people's minds'.[11] In this model all Christian believers can be context theologians. The process of interpretation evaluates cultural experience against the Christians' experience of God. Bevans outlines several advantages to this model. Firstly, it is a new way of doing theology – theology as activity. The historical and the cultural are genuine sources of revelation. The universal structure of human knowing and consciousness provides a common ground for mutual conversation and interaction. The model has however not been without it criticisms.

As Bevans indicates, some have criticized the process as too abstract and difficult to grasp. The assumption of the universality of human knowing has been questioned. It may be that such a view is a western male assumption. The greatest danger of a subjective focus is that experience-led revelation may degenerate into relativity and utilitarian individualism, the very process that we are trying to find an alternative to. Having mentioned this, the general approach of this book to emphasize that all of God's self-revelation is realized in the context of subjective human experience, and this is a core understanding of the Cappadocian Fathers and now, of postmodern theology. I can see now through researching this book, that different emerging Church communities are utilizing different models of contextual theology. Those of a more trinitarian influenced ecclesiology seem to be utilizing a transcendent model, whilst those more attentive to culture and emerging faith, are utilizing a synthetic model. Both however, stand quite opposed to what Bevans calls the 'translation model' of contextual theology favoured by those of a more conservative, fundamentalist sensibility. This form of theological engagement conforms to Niebuhr's 'Christ against culture', where 'culture' is seen negatively as a distraction from Christ.[12] As a model of contextual theology, the translation approach emphasizes retaining

---

[11] Bevans, *Models*, 100-4.
[12] H R Niebuhr *Christ and culture*, (New York: Harper & Row, 1951), 30-9.

Christian identity, as dictated by tradition, as more important than cultural identity. There is little awareness or acceptance that with this model, the church needs to be immersed in a particular culture.[13] This approach could be accused of window dressing or *sexing-up* the faith, where externally it may appear updated, but remains essentially unchanged. Rather than being a subjective 'I-Thou' encounter, revelation is more about communication of certain unchanging absolute truths or doctrines of God, and because they are from God they are wholly culturally free.[14] As Bevans says, there is a real danger of over emphasizing knowledge of God through facts rather than God's self-revelatory presence:

> *We might criticize as well the translation model's implicit notion of revelation as propositional. Revelation is not just a message from God, a list of truths that Christians must believe. Revelation is the manifestation of God's presence in human life and human society, and the Bible represents the written record of that manifestation in particular times and within a particular society... the texts of the Bible are the results not of heavenly dictation, but of the struggles of women and men of faith to make sense out of that faith in the midst of lives where God's presence was often less than self-evident. Rather than a list of doctrines to be believed, the Bible – and to some extent the Christian tradition – presents various valid ways of wrestling with faith and doing theology.*[15]

It is this absolutising abuse of the creeds (such as the Nicene Creed) and defining who is in and who is out, that makes many contemporary Christians weary of dogma and the early creeds. But rather than give up the gift of the Cappadocian Fathers wisdom, many of us remain committed to the use of models, such as the transcendent approach, which help to inform the ongoing process of subjective understanding of the self-revealing God, and the deep truth of Trinitarian theology. Rather than fear culture and difference, we are called to trust that God is very much present in our world and in our culture. The way we live this out will hopefully enable fundamentalists to understand that there are other ways of being Christian in the world.

---

[13] Bevans, *Models*, 30-46.
[14] Bevans, *Models*, 34.
[15] Bevans, *Models*, 37.

Trinitarian presence in places you least expect
One of my dearest friends consistently challenges me about being too comfortably Christian. He is a self-confessed Unitarian, who is on his own very particular Christian-based journey. He reminds me, like Pete Rollins, that if we are sincere about the transcendent God, and the apophatic tradition, then we need to ensure that we are not just attending to what we know and are comfortable with, but to those things which are uncomfortable and disorientating, trusting that God is in the mix somewhere. So when approaching the bible, we don't just look at the bits we know we like to back up what we already think, but we need to attend to those bits that enrage and frustrate us. In a Church I used to attend, you would have been forgiven for thinking that the Bible consisted only of the New Testament, and that letters of St Paul were really the only parts worth reading. It was all far too simplistic and comfortable. Part of the calling of emerging Churches is not to run away from complex issues, and to live with a high regard for inclusive love, social and ecological justice. This is called orthopraxis, so that life is not just about right thinking (orthodoxy) but about how this informs the way we live (orthopraxis).

This really hits home for me, when we start talking about people I feel threatened by. Being very frank, this includes: aggressive and abusive homeless people, alcoholics, racists, Islamic, Hindu, Jewish and Christian religious fundamentalists, those who demean women, and those who are homophobic. These are my top six hates. If I truly believe in this transcendent God of perichoresis, kenosis and panentheism, I need to be open to the possibility that this same God can be made present to such people. Can I trust God enough to make the divine present to these people? Do I truly believe that God is seeking to draw all things into restored relationship with the divine? Or to put it another way, do I believe that Christ, as the image (ikon) of the invisible God, is self-revealed in all contexts, and beckons all people towards the Trinitarian God? This is hinted strongly in Colossians:

> *He is the image [ikon] of the invisible God, the firstborn of all creation. For by him all things were created: things in heaven and on earth, visible and invisible, whether thrones or powers or rulers or authorities; all things were created by him and for him. He is before all things, and in him all things hold together.*
> Colossians 1:15-17

This is profound and challenging stuff. If you remember in Chapter One, the Cappadocians utilise this idea of the 'image' or the ikon of God to justify their argument of the three persons of God as the three images of God in one being. Scripture suggests that God illuminates the truth of God's nature through image. So how far is God illuminated in human experience outside of those I feel comfortable with?

Following this text to its logical conclusion, should we not understand that all things encounter the Trinitarian nature of God, even fundamentalists and those from other faith traditions? Even those I would naturally exclude? It was the insight of a shared transcendent experience that enabled the various Christian traditions of the charismatic renewal in the 1960's and 1970's to come together. They realised that God transcended difference through Holy Spirit-led, self-revealed activity. God challenges us in those profound places of difference and discomfort, unsettling us, encouraging us into encounter with the divine that knows no bounds. This is one of the reasons the Moot Community (inspired by Ikon, a sister emerging church community), went to a conservative Zionist Synagogue in London. We hoped to be transcendently challenged by the encounter. This book came out of that encounter.

So how is the Holy Trinity to be found present in unsurprising places? Well firstly, I was surprised to find strong Trinitarian understandings in some Christian fundamentalist writings. Haleblian outlines three doctrines considered basic to Christian orthodoxy, which he believed were in some way universally true for all people throughout all of history.[16] Even in this very black and white approach there is an acknowledgement that the Trinity 'articulates best what God is truly like and what faith in God means for life in the world.'[17] More controversially is the question, how is the Holy Trinity made present in other world religions?

Richard Sudworth reminds us, as the title of his new book suggests, that the Triune God is *Distinctly Welcoming*, and is present in our current 21st century, multi-faith society. Even in the complexity of such a society, the God of the Trinity beckons:

> *The concept of God's mission, not ours...should be no surprise to us...God is God and will move, by his Spirit, speaking to*

---

[16] K Haleblian, "*The Problem of Contextualization*," Missiology, XI, 1 (January, 1983):101-2.
[17] Ibid.

> *people, engineering encounters, listening to the cries and prayers of all sorts of odd outsiders in ways that God is completely at liberty to. This foundation of mission is, I believe, crucial to our understanding of other faiths. Once we see God, untamed, unconfined, working in and beyond the church, the way we approach and pray for others will inevitably shift.*[18]

Sudworth's perspective is transcendent, believing that God's nature as Trinity, and the particular role of the Sustainer, means that the Trinity can be 'imaged' within any and all faiths, as God draws all to restored relationship with the divine. Sudworth suggests that the belief in God as triune is core to the Christian faith. Therefore, God exists in community, and intends for us to live and work in relationship. As a result, a strong, caring community should be the focus and aim of the work we do. The desire to create community is therefore driven by the triune God in us.[19] If this is true, then God is drawing all to experience the subjective truths the self-revealing God conveys. Sudworth again:

> *In one sense, the concept of the Trinity underpins all the hallmarks of our distinctive faith. The Creator God is the Father, the Eternal Word and the Spirit. We understand God through the incarnation of his Son, and we in turn are called to incarnate the life of Christ through the Spirit. The redeeming nature of God is demonstrated in the cross where death is defeated and where all humanity can turn to obtain new life in the Spirit. God's grace is manifest in the Son, full of grace and truth, and of the Spirit. We can trust in the resurrection of the dead and the newness of all things because the Father raised the Son from death and his Spirit is poured out on believers as a sign and promise of the new creation to come. God's covenant with us is established in the blood of the cross of his Son and sealed in us by the presence of the Spirit. Belief in a 'Triune God' is therefore something more than abstract and mystifying theology but the kernel of the Christian faith.*[20]

Although Orthodox Judaism and Islam traditionally view the Greek theological understanding of the Trinity as puzzling and even blasphemous, it is interesting that both these religions have mystical

---

[18] R Sudworth, *Distinctly Welcoming*, (Bletchley, UK: SCP, 2007), 29.
[19] Sudworth, *Distinctly,* 48-9.
[20] Sudworth, *Distinctly,* 71-2.

traditions that draw on an understanding of the Spirit and the immanence of God. Both Kabbalah in Judaism and Sufism in Islam resonate with the ideas of kenosis and panentheism – the idea of an immanent God, present in our world. Although they could never believe in a Triune God, they can believe in the One-God having the attributes of Creator, Redeemer and Companion.

Kabbalah draws heavily on the rabbinical form of the faith created in the times of the Babylonian exile. Yahweh had been seen as the transcendent Creator God, but after the exile and destruction of the temple, was seen as a God in their midst.[21] In the very earliest passages of the Talmud, God was experienced in mysterious physical phenomena. The Rabbis spoke about the Holy Spirit, which had brooded over creation and the building of the sanctuary, making Gods presence felt in a rushing wind or a blazing fire.[22] Kabbalists have traditionally understood that the Spirit makes God present through mystical, subjective experience. Whilst in exile, Jews held to the idea of Shekinah, the glory of God. It is derived from the Hebrew *shakan*, meaning 'to dwell with' or 'to pitch tent'. Therefore the Shekinah of God was mystically present with them wherever they were:

> *The image of the Shekinah helped the exiles to cultivate a sense of God's presence wherever they were. The Rabbis spoke of the Shekinah skipping from one synagogue of the Diaspora to another; others said that it stood at the door of the synagogue, blessing each step that a Jew took on his way to the House of Studies...*[23]

This mystically present God, related to Yahweh and the Holy Spirit, has remained a key concept in Kabbalah, the focus being the cultivation of a sense of God within each human being so that their dealings with others became sacred encounters.[24] Now if we believe that the Triune God becomes transcendently accessible to all things including of faith traditions, we can understand this insight as the work of God. God, who is 'before all things', can be seen as drawing all to an understanding of the Trinity through the inspiration of the Holy Spirit.

---

[21] K Armstrong, *A History of God,* (London: Vintage, 1999), 90-1.
[22] Armstrong, *A History,* 91.
[23] Armstrong, *A History* ,95.
[24] Armstrong, *A History,* 97.

Sufi's believe that al-Lah is the absolute, and alone has true existence.[25] Rabiah, an early Sufi prophetess, wrote about al-Lah as a God of Love who desired an intimate, redemptive relationship with all human beings.[26] Sufis had a high view of God and Christ, professing that 'There is no god but al-Lah and Jesus is his Messenger'.[27] Al-Lah is seen as a sustaining presence in the universe. So again you could argue that the Triune God has transcendently brought these truths to the more mystical expressions of Islam through mystical encounter.

Both Sufism and Kabbalah emphasise a kenotic understanding of God, whereby love is poured out into all existence. This creative and salvific action reveals God's presence.[28] With such a focus on the love of God, God's sustaining presence in the world, Kenosis and the Holy Spirit, there is plenty of common ground for fruitful dialogue between progressive Muslims, Christians and Jews.

I am not saying here that all religions lead to the same God. I am saying that God is mystically present to all things, and that we can have confidence that God is seeking to draw all things back into restored relationship with the Triune God, and that God will do what God will do. This transcendent and incarnational understanding of God's mission to the world, requires us to hold a more mystical and trusting understanding. Mission and evangelism is not about us representing the absent God; it is much more about us trying to catch up with what God is already doing. Just as God used the charismatic renewal to bring deeper understanding of the Trinity to the Western church, the mystical God uses the Holy Spirit to draw other religions to the truths of God, through subjective experience. Western Christianity must learn from that of the East, and begin to practice this more loving approach to the world's religions, and then just maybe, we will stop crusading against a perceived enemy, seeking instead to love people hoping that people will encounter God through our actions and activities out of hospitality and self-sacrifice. Here's hoping!!

The Trinity has had a profound influence on the socio-political level also, challenging the status quo, for example in South America. In the late 1960's to 1990's, understandings of the Trinity concerning social and ecological justice became keenly felt in places of significant poverty and oppression. Jurgen Moltmann, writing in 1967, and Leonardo Boff in 1976, both drew on a relational model of the Trinity

---

[25] Ibid 180
[26] ibid 265-7
[27] ibid.
[28] ibid 157.

and the implications of perichoresis and panentheism, to argue for the unity and relational connectedness of all things.[29] Humanity should seek to incarnate the equality modeled within the Godhead on a societal level.[30] Liberation theologies stress Jesus prioritization toward the poor and oppressed, and emphasize doing theology in specific social, political, and economic contexts. Jesus treated the poor preferentially, so this new theological methodology also gave priority to the poor. The idea of orthopraxis, or 'right action', came out of this commitment to practical love. Jesus wasn't merely a lovely person; he acted lovingly, challenged people, went to parties, and always included those who were poor or marginalized.

Further, out of this understanding of panentheism and Trinitarianism, Boff made significant advances when considering ecological justice. In the 1990's Boff sought, in a series of works on ecology, "to connect the cry of the oppressed with the cry of the earth."[31] In his understanding, an ecological liberation theology is a multi-dimensional project that seeks the welfare of people and the planet.[32]

Trinitarian theology radically challenges not only the Christian faith, but also other religions, and oppression and injustice throughout the world, even on the ecological level. It is quite awe inspiring what has been made possible by the self-revealing God, who through the Holy Spirit, has given all things access to an experience of the transcendent, beckoning them into restored relationship.

Emerging Churches: Commitment to the pursuit of transcendent, contextual theology

An emphasis upon transcendent encounter is prevalent within the emerging Church, as is the practice of debate and dialogue as the method of exploration and knowledge acquisition. These are participative opportunities for people to explore, grapple and seek meaning. Alternative worship is an interesting medium for the seeking of transcendence. Often its services have 'stations' which are opportunities for encounter, and for exploration of the various concepts

---

[29] L Boff, *Liberating Grace*, (MaryKnoll, New York: Orbis, 1979).

[30] J Moltmann, *Theology of hope; on the ground and the implications of a Christian eschatology*. Translated by James W. Leitch, (London, SCM Press, 1967).

[31] L Boff, *Cry of the Poor, Cry of the Earth*, (Maryknoll, New York: Orbis Books, 1997).

[32] Ibid.

raised. This is all very much within the context of an active relationship with the transcendent God.

> *Much of the energy in the emerging church scene centres on energizing worship and reviving ancient practices, often seen as more genuine, raw and meaningful. The goal: a more "biblical" church. Emerging worshippers value mystery, transcendence and the experience of communion.*[33]

In so doing, as we explored earlier in Chapter 4, the emerging Church has found a more ancient understanding of the idea of sacrament: the Spirit has made God present within each of us, so we are sacraments of God as we engage with the world. All life, by its very nature is sacramental. This means that 'church', when understood as occurring in sacramental moments, happens whenever two or three people are gathered together. This may be over a pint of bitter at the local pub, whenever and wherever people pray together, or when people involve themselves in social justice. These expressions of sacramentality are moments when God can transcendently express the divine in our lives. This refreshingly earthed understanding asserts that God is very present at all times and in all places. This is after all, how I became a Christian in a nightclub, and how the Apostle Paul became a Christian travelling on a road.

Some Alternative worship groups and emerging Churches have been exploring the use of 'Godly Play' as a medium of worship and transcendent, Christian meaning making. This is an approach to telling bible stories that leaves room for participants to explore the story through the use of 'Wonderment Questioning'. This enables people to place themselves in the story and explore meaning. So rather than taking a Sunday School approach of expecting people to know God through learning 'facts about God', it takes a transcendent, contextual approach that uses questioning to enable people to know God through transcendent experience. It is based on the ancient visual and oral art of story telling, and brings awe, mystery and enchantment. To illustrate the power of this approach let me share an experience.

On a visit to a small emerging Church group in New Zealand, I wanted to test out the power of Godly Play, by doing it in a different culture. With the use of a sandpit and some basic props, I told half of

---

[33] As recorded on the world wide web as downloaded on the 14th January 2007 http://www.religionlink.org/tip_060410.php

the story of Abraham and Sarah, up to the point that they wander around the desert. I stopped telling the story near the end, to allow people to ask wonderment questions. Around the sandpit sat children with their parents, one of whom kicked off saying, "I wonder what it was like to hear God's voice?" I replied, "I wonder?' After a little while, a girl no more than six years old said, "I wonder what it is like to be a woman following a man who hears the voice of a God you cannot hear?" Again I replied, "I wonder?" People were profoundly moved by this insight, which inspired all present to engage deeper with the meaning of the story. Later still, a small boy asked, "I wonder what it is like to trust the voice of enough God to move out of town?" I replied, "I wonder why you think Abraham had to trust God to move out of town?" To which he replied, "I wonder if I would ever trust God enough to give up what I have?" The power in this approach for questing for spiritual meaning is self-evident. I am always profoundly moved when I am involved in Godly Play. On this occasion I dutifully finished the story, people then painted what they had learnt, shared a snack meal and a prayer, and then left. If that is not profoundly inclusive and open-ended church, then I don't know what is.

Jerome Berryman, the creator of Godly Play, makes connections between the story telling, wondering and responding of Godly Play with the ancient practice of *lectio divina*. This form of worship was developed by Christian monastic communities as a spiritual discipline of holy reading, meditation, prayer and responding to scriptural texts.[34] The reader came to the text to seek an intuitive understanding, to grow in wisdom, to savour the aesthetic value of the words, and ultimately to encounter God, all of which is very similar to Godly Play. Godly Play therefore has strong similarities to pre-enlightenment modes of thinking and knowing. It is not about objective data or the scientific method, which rejects subjective knowledge as myth and fantasy.[35] Rather it is about re-contextualizing the place of subjective experience as a way of knowing. God is made present via the Holy Spirit within the sacramental and transcendent moment. In my view, Taylor gives the best explanation for what is going on in Godly Play. In 2 Corinthians 3:16-18, we understand that when people turn to the Lord 'the veil is removed', which is freedom.[36] 'The LORD' of whom this passage speaks is the Holy Spirit, and the result of that clear vision of Jesus

---

[34] J W Berryman, *The Complete Guide to Godly Play Volume 3,* (Denver: Living the Good News Publishing, 2002), 19, 21-22.
[35] Ibid, 21-2.
[36] Note: Translation taken from the NRSV.

Christ is that we ourselves begin to be changed 'into the same image'[37] as Christ. The focus of the text is then thrown onto the end of verse eighteen, 'for this comes from the Lord, the Spirit'. As Taylor says, the relationship between the Holy Spirit and Christ, is by now indistinguishable.[38] The Holy Spirit is dynamically involved in the gap between us, both as individuals and as communities, and God. Taylor has called the Holy Spirit the *Go Between God* to reflect this. God the Holy Spirit is instrumental in the development of the 'I Thou' relationship.[39] It is in this context that we understand the Holy Spirit as the counselor that Jesus talked about, who would follow after him and guide Christians in all truth.[40]

When drawn into relationship by the Triune God, our natural response is to try to connect with what we experience as an elusive presence.[41] We cannot fully capture our experience of God in any activity, story or rite, yet God's presence continually invites us to follow the glimpses disclosed through the Holy Spirit in sacramental moments.

The importance of *Godly Play* or *lectio divina*, is the involvement of the Holy Spirit in these activities of worship. God the Spirit draws our attention to Christ, in whom alone the meaning of personhood is fully revealed. This drawing of our attention began at Pentecost and has continued to this day.[42] It is this openness to attention that enables Christians to know God through experience. As Taylor states:

> *True attention is an involuntary self-surrender to the object of the attention. The Holy Spirit is that power which opens eyes that are closed, hearts that are unaware and minds that shrink from too much reality. If one is open to towards God, one is open also to the beauty of the world.*[43]

This sacramental understanding is ultimately expressed in table fellowship and the Eucharist, and it is profoundly exciting that so many emerging Church groups have such a high regard for these practices. It

---

[37] Note: Some translations are more explicitly "into his likeness".
[38] J V Taylor, *The Go Between God*, (London: SCM, 1975), 107-110.
[39] Ibid, 8.
[40] John 14: 15-27.
[41] Berryman, *The Complete 1*, 25-26.
[42] Taylor, *The Go*, 107-117, 199.
[43] Taylor, *The Go*, 18-19.

has always amused me that the Moot Community's Eucharist Services are generally the best attended. Their fusion of alternative worship and the ancient rite of the Eucharist, truly brings transcendent experience. Such services are Ancient:future places where God is free to do what God will do through the divine nature of Kenotic love.

A commitment to transcendent spiritual pursuits implies a high regard to coming together as a community. Emerging Churches tend to see community as the reflection of God's nature, and it therefore receives significant emphasis. In the next chapter we will be addressing the importance of the discovery of identity, both personal and communal, through the medium of intentional community.

Reflection
We have really pushed the boat out in this chapter, saying that what God models in perichoresis influences not only how we are church, but also political, environmental and social circumstances. This takes us into new territory, territory often conceived of as off-limits by previous generations of Christians, and many fundamentalists in our own age. However, God empowers us with the ability and the insight to catch up with whatever God is up to in all spheres of human existence and social organisation. Indeed this now involves going beyond human existence itself, and reaching out to the whole of created matter. Without an understanding of the Trinity, it would be impossible to conceive of how it all relates in the transcendent power of God.

Chapter Seven

The challenge of human community in a culture of individualism

New Years Eve is often a time of taking stock of the year just passed, and giving consideration, or even making resolutions for the year ahead. It was in this spirit that, at a recent New Years Eve party, someone asked me what I most longed for in life. As well as the usual wishes - partner, health and happiness – my friend was surprised to hear me say, 'and to live in a large enough house so I could set up an intentional spiritual community with close friends and others'. Ever since my student days, I have lived in accommodation that catered for multiple occupants, and I have always loved it. One of the strengths of the alternative worship movement were the many students that, living in shared accommodation, helped energise whatever was going on. From its inception, the alternative worship movement, and the subsequent emerging Church movement in the UK, has had a strong emphasis on community. As we explored earlier, many in our contemporary culture crave relational intimacy in community, and yet fear it in equal measure.[1] This idealised desire for belonging in community goes very deep, but where does it come from? The reality of life in the 21st century is that it is largely an individualistic pursuit. In fact, we often assume that people are able to choose the communal life if they so desired, but I am not sure that this is really the case. Many of us have grown up in a culture of extreme individualism and independence, the secular mantra of our parent's generation. This has resulted in many of us being rendered utterly unskilled when it comes to communal life, which is about giving, taking, and tolerance - particularly of those you do not like. In a culture of individualistic consumerism, doing and being community is quite a challenge. You can observe this lack of social skills when people are required to negotiate shared space, like public transport. Some have no idea about considering the needs of others, whether it be in queuing, in giving up a seat for a disabled or elderly person, getting on or off the bus, or listening to music (especially if you happen to have a loud speaker on your cell phone!). The individual reigns supreme, and with little regard to others. It is all about taking with little regard to giving.

In chapter 5 we explored how many in today's culture define the 'self' through patterns of consumption, which is in turn informed by information technology. Factors such as place, work and family are increasingly irrelevant in the formation of identity. Theologically, the challenge for community starts with a concern for what it means to be an individual human being. The biblical narrative of the 'covenanted being', which lies at the core of the Judeo-Christian belief system, is quite different from the pic 'n' mix, consumerist approach to personal identification. But what is this personal covenanted identity?

Brueggemann draws on the concept of the 'covenanted self' to explore personal development from a biblical perspective.[2] He draws on the Psalms and the prophecy of Amos[3] to explore how the Israelites were covenanted to God's 'otherness'.[4] Brueggemann defines covenant as 'a theological commitment ... to be enacted as a mode of shared life' and as 'a covenant commitment between God, individuals and groups of people.'[5] By implication personal identity is drawn from an understanding of the self in God. Brueggemann interprets this to be a

---

[1] Z Bauman, *Liquid Modernity*, (Cambridge: Polity Press, 2000), 100-6.
[2] W. Brueggemann, *The Covenanted Self, Explorations in law and covenant.* (Minneapolis: Fortress Press, 1999).
[3] See Psalm 139:7-12, Amos 9:2-4.
[4] Brueggemann, *Covenanted*, 2.
[5] ibid,1, 37-9.

radical alternative to our contextual postmodern 'consumption informed identity' which he perceives as debilitating Christians and the Church.[6] He challenges the key psychological assumption of individualistic independence, in that from a Judaeo-Christian perspective the 'human-self' is never an isolated or autonomous being, but always and necessarily preceded by God's 'thou'.[7] Therefore the Christian assumption should be that God has evoked, summoned, authorized, and 'faithed' us into existence as person's. Brueggemann concurs with the psychological concept of *life stage development* because it connotes the sense of life as a journey of personal-identity formation. In this sense 'human beings' can be considered 'human becomings'.[8] Therefore, building a self-concept and world-view is less a matter of consumer choice, and more about engaging with God's otherness – the 'thou', which constantly inspires and undermines who we may choose to be. Spiritually understood, personal development is more of an enterprise of coming to terms with this 'other' or 'thou' in a way that is neither excessively submissive nor resistant. As with the Psalms, the presence of the *other* always reminds us that we are addressed, unsettled, unfinished, underway, and not fully whom we intend or pretend to be. Brueggemann explores Winnicott's theory of emotional development, which addresses the consequences of maternal parenting on the child's life stage development.[9] Brueggemann interprets the outcomes of various life stages to and with a covenanted solution. For example, in early life, the development of a healthy relationship between mother and child enables a dual capacity to assert and to yield in the mother-child relationship. A healthy outcome would be a covenanting with intimacy. Covenanting is therefore a process, with God, with others, and with the self.[10]

This process of the 'othering' of the self enables a covenanted identity to be formed that resources a healthy self-understanding in the

---

[6] ibid, 1.
[7] ibid, 1-2.
[8] ibid, 3-6.
[9] D. W. Winnicott, 1971, *The Maturational Processes and the Facilitating Environment: Studies in the Theory of Emotional Development*, (London: Tavistock Press), as recorded in W. Bruggemann, *Covenanted*, 3-6.
[10] As Brueggemann details, with God – complaint and hymn, assertion of self and abandonment of self, with Neighbours – joy and sorrow, truth in love, up-building in the midst of freedom, With the Self – readiness to receive scattering and the freedom for gathering a self that is unlike the old one, a process of conversion and transformation. Brueggemann, *Covenanted*, 16.

context of others.[11] However, life remains an experience of ups and downs. Brueggemann draws on the Psalms to see how the Israelites coped with the struggle of survival in a chaotic and threatening world. His analysis of the Psalms reveals a pattern of orientation – disorientation – reorientation, in response to various changes and crises.[12] In the midst of such constant change, individual identity relates to the process of the 'gathered-self' working through cyclical experiences of orientation, disorientation to reorientation; or, as Bauman would say, a process of dis-embedding and re-embedding. Lament Psalms express an appeal to God to make things right in a crisis. This is a full assertion of the self over God - "Where are you God?" - followed sometimes by a faith that God "will remain with us" even though times are difficult. Lament occurs in times of disorientation. The process works through to the sense of reorientation found in the Praise Psalms, where praise is the full abandonment of self to God. The experience of God in times of orientation, disorientation and reorientation, coupled with the experience of God through prayer, worship and teaching, all assist in the formation of self-identity covenanted to God's otherness. This process then continues in cycles of 'I-Thou' discovery. As Brueggemann states, God is a transcendent mystery that will not go away.[13] He sees the covenanted process as deeply embedding for individuals living in a threatening world. Such a process of identity formation is a radical alternative to the dis-embedding reality of our social context.

Volf reminds us that the 'I-thou' relationship with God fully accommodates our uniqueness as individual human beings:

> *It is precisely the uniqueness of God's relation to me that makes me into a unique person. Yet in God's relation to me, a relation creating me as an individual human being, I do not stand as an individual isolated from other human beings and my environment. An isolated individual of this sort does not exist. Human beings are in actuality imbedded in a network of multiple and diverse social and natural relationships; this applies not only to newborn infants, who have not yet become subjects, but even to solitary ascetics, who do, after all, live a spiritually real communion and must draw their sustenance from nature... God's own relationship with human beings, a relationship that first*

---

[11] Brueggemann draws on Psalm 103 to make this connection.
[12] Brueggemann, *Covenanted*, 14-19.
[13] *Ibid*, 3.

> *constitutes a human being into a person, always realises itself through the differentiated existence of every person in these multiple relations...Without other human beings, even God cannot create a human being! Even if God were to create an isolated being, that being would not be a human being.*[14]

Fascinatingly, Volf makes a connection with this and the wording of the Genesis 1:27 text we looked at in chapter 1:

> *This may be the anthropological significance of the peculiar transition in Gen 1:27 from singular to plural: "So God created humankind in his image, in the image of God he created him; male and female he created them".*[15]

By implication, our encounter with the Trinity is as unique human individuals. It is the Creator who leads the perichoresis who mysteriously institutes us as unique human beings, and it is the participation of the Redeemer through the Spirit in co-operation with human community, that constitutes us as human beings. People then have freedom to realise this connection with God and/or human community, or to reject it. This sense of constitution goes even deeper with all those who have chosen to realise the Christian faith as their story.

Here in our personal interiority we find deep connection with the Holy Spirit – the unfathomable mystery of God's indwelling - informing of our self-identity.[16] Volf goes further to suggest that it is Christ who, recognising our individual uniqueness, draws us together to realise our common-unity.

> *The Spirit present in all Christians "opens" each of them to all others. It starts them on the way to creative mutual giving and receiving, in which each grows in her or his unique way and all have joy in one another.*[17]

Here we see the importance of the inter-relatedness of God, the individual person, and community. Throughout this book we have explored the implications of the perichoresis, the interpenetration of the

---

[14] M Volf, *After Our Likeness*, 182-3.
[15] *Ibid*, 183.
[16] *Ibid*, 188.
[17] *Ibid*, 189.

three persons of the Godhead, which goes far beyond what we can conceive. We have explored how church that is modelled on the Trinity lives through the participation of its members, who are themselves constituted by the Holy Spirit. The triune God, who through the Holy Spirit is made present, interpenetrates each of us as unique human beings. Therefore community becomes an important environment for the realisation of our unique potential. The place of Church, as the alternative loving and inclusive community reflecting the invisible Kingdom of God, then becomes the highest expression of this community that loves people into their potential. The place of community then is key.

It is unsurprising then to find, that if the constituting effects of community which enable the individual to fully develop are not present or are disrupted, the individual is unable to realise the fullness of their potential. As I explored in my first book, and more briefly in the previous chapter, our post-industrial western society is characterised by fluidity, and the hugely significant shift from communities built around 'place' to those of 'network'. As a result of the fluidity of network communities, relationships are constantly changing, particularly in urban areas. It becomes extremely difficult in this context, to be constituted as a human being, to realise your potential. As social relating has been dramatically affected by consumption, married and unmarried relationships cease to be 'for ever', and tend to be determined more by perceived happiness and personal fulfilment. In the UK, we have not recovered from the way community was threatened and even despised the late 1970's and 1980's. This was epitomised by the then Prime Minister Margaret Thatcher who said:

> *There's no such thing as society. There are individual men and women and there are families. And no government can do anything except through people, and people must look after themselves first.*[18]

For quite a while in the UK, the idea of community has been neglected in favour of a self-centred personal responsibility. Since then the UK has become one of largest economic centres of the world, but has also consistently been one of the worst countries with regard to poverty and child deprivation. There is also an increasingly large gap between the incomes of richest and poorest in the country. In a culture

---

[18] http://en.wikiquote.org/wiki/Margaret_Thatcher

centred on the individual, there has been significant neglect at a community level.

Currently, many of the UK's urban contexts suffer from problems associated with the absence of parents, particularly fathers, in a culture of ever increasing under age sex and teen parenthood. Young people are under enormous pressure in our new highly tested and highly sexualised culture. It is no surprise then, that the post-industrial, postmodern West has seen an exponential rise in suicides, mental illness, homelessness, relationship breakdown and stress.

As we explored in the last chapter, there is a huge desire for deeper forms of personal identity, a hunger for inner peace and happiness. Many have such a poor sense of personal identity, that they don't realise their need for God. The church as ekklesia, the alternative community, a visible and yet incomplete sign of God's Kingdom, must enable people to achieve their potential as 'human becomings' through the constituting effects of community and covenant with God. So how is this possible?

In many alternative worship groups and emerging Churches the sense of community is very strong. There is a commitment to support, encouragement and mutual learning. In my research of emerging and Fresh Expressions of Church, it was evident that many of these projects encounter people as spiritual tourists seeking spiritual meaning and community. This questing leads people to check out these communities, sometimes staying on the edge of events for one to two years before getting fully involved. With an emphasis on 'belonging before believing', many look to the emerging Church for the opportunity to explore their identity and their need for God. It is unsurprising that many emerging churches draw heavily on the wisdom of pastoral carers, spiritual directors, mental health workers, psychiatrists, social workers, therapists and psychologists. All these assist emerging churches to achieve communities of health and wellness. Committed friendships are built up; we learn to open up about our lives and struggles, often learning from the experience of others. Most importantly, community is an opportunity to learn how to tolerate people who are different or challenging. It also aids in the patterning of ones life, so as to be able to turn up reliably at events. We learn to trust, to listen, to give, and in short, to reach our potential. In this way, the Trinitarian God, through the constitution of identity, strengthens incomplete church communities, enabling us to model the beauty of perichoresis, and therefore, human becoming in community. The similarities between these forms of church and 'therapeutic communities' are significant.[19] Both have regular community governance meetings that promote ownership of the community. Tasks are shared, and new people are supported and socialised into the community. Leadership is flat and modelled as servanthood and participation. In this way participants have their uniqueness as individuals affirmed and begin to realise their potential. And of course, community inculcates an awareness of others who must also be encouraged in the same way. This is after all the strength of the 'mystical communion model' we identified in Chapter Four. A whole of life approach to discipleship and catechesis is also essential. The Beta Course and Soul Sparks are but two very good examples of this.[20]

It is important that the Church realise that people no longer come fully skilled and able to engage with community. Many carry unresolved psychological and social issues; many are struggling with stress, anxiety and depression. Many are confused about who they are, or are carry deep issues of personal doubt or self-loathing. All of which will be projected into the life, relationships, hopes and dreams of the spiritual community they attend, if not dealt with adaptively. This is why so many churches are terribly dysfunctional. Our hope has to be that if we really face up to these difficulties, they can be addressed and we can have healthy, adaptive co-journeying communities.

The Moot Community, of which I am part, has promoted the use of external spiritual directors, mentors, counsellors, and is now considering running a stress and contemplative prayer course, soon to be trialled. We seek to emulate the complexity of the perichoretic Triune Godhead by recognising the interconnectedness of personal identity, health, church and spirituality. Any attempt to do Church as worship, mission and community must offer places for people to find themselves, to learn life skills and find health, as well as exploring the narratives of the Christian faith. One key asset in this endeavour is the place of contemplative prayer. Generally speaking, a form of spirituality that is cognitively 'true' is of less importance than one that 'works'. Many are willing to try anything if there's a chance it will bring stillness, peace and centeredness to the stress and restlessness experienced in everyday life. The ancient Christian contemplative tradition is the perfect resource for meeting the very real, personal needs of today. I witnessed the potency of this contemplative approach at the Mind, Body and Spirit festival stall mentioned earlier. Here, short

---

[19] http://en.wikipedia.org/wiki/Therapeutic_community
[20] http://www.course.soulspark.org.uk, http://www.beta-course.org/

introductory approaches to contemplative prayer opened up whole vistas of opportunity for those spiritual tourists who tried it. Some found centeredness and peace, and experiences of authentic transcendence, through openness to spiritual encounter. Others cried in relief of getting beyond pain; others expressed joy at getting beyond restlessness. It is my hope that they continued using these effective contemplative approaches to Christianity.

It is not just alternative worship groups, and emerging and Fresh Expressions of church who have found this approach to work: it has also been effective in the corporate business world:

> *Corporate executives seek opportunities for silent retreats. Major businesses add meditation rooms to the workplace environment. Women and men earning impressive salaries quit their jobs to find a quieter pace, a more peaceful environment, a closer connection with the land, a greater sense of purpose.*[21]

In her profound essay, *Spirituality in a Postmodern Era*, McCarthy identifies contemplative awareness as essential to the development of authentic spirituality. In her view, authentic spirituality is that which "works", in that it makes connections with the restless, searching nature of spiritual tourists.

> *Authentic spirituality is grounded in the discipline of contemplative awareness. Awareness as a discipline opens us to levels of reality not immediately apparent. It enables us to see ourselves, our circumstances, our world without illusion... It requires stillness, receptivity, and availability. The discipline of awareness involves deep listening, which is marked by waiting, attending, and presence. We must sit in the stillness, wait, and listen deeply. And we must be silent. The discipline of contemplative awareness is nurtured in the practice of silence. We consciously create pools of silence in which to hear. We quiet the many voices around us and within us as we wait to hear a word of revelation...Contemplative awareness does not lead to withdrawal from the world, but a deep immersion in the world. One becomes more aware of and attentive to the realms of everyday life, to the joys and sorrows, the sufferings and*

---

[21] M McCarthy, *Spirituality in a Postmodern Era*, in J Woodward S Pattison (eds.) *The Blackwell Reader in Pastoral and Practical Theology*, (Oxford: Blackwell, 2000),193-4.

> *ecstasies, the struggles and triumphs of very real people in very real circumstances...Authentic spirituality, then, is marked by dynamic relationship between contemplation and action which works toward the healing of the world and wellbeing of all creation.*[22]

This extremely ancient approach to prayer and contemplation provides an opportunity for the meeting of God and humans, through the power of the imagination. It is part of a long tradition that dates from the early Christian mystics, through to the contemplatives and charismatics of today. However the practices involved in contemplative prayer aren't known as disciplines for nothing – they require application and diligence. In our culture of instant gratification, learning this is going to be hard work. However, one can learn simple techniques that gradually equip the user to then go deeper. The Moot Community now aim to include contemplative approaches to prayer in most services, and take the opportunity to conduct workshops and seminars on a regular basis. Something that must be borne in mind when developing the contemplative prayer life, is that a balance must be struck between being alone and being community. It can become an overly individualistic pursuit, with the result that we shy away from community. As we have already seen, such a situation makes it very difficult to realise our potential. McCarthy again puts this better than I could:

> *Grounding in a community of discourse, belief, and practice is a further feature of authentic spirituality. We do not undertake the spiritual quest alone. We need communities which nurture and hold us, communities which keep traditions and charisms alive and which hand them on to the next generation. Because we are human beings, we most often come an encounter with the sacred through the mediation of the traditions, practices, and charisms of particular spiritual traditions. And these traditions and charisms take root, develop, and are handed on only in the context of a community that keeps them alive. Thus an individual, privatized, or purely personal spirituality is an oxymoron. Authentic spirituality can never be an isolated, privatized, individual affair. It is always located in a particular*

---

[22] Ibid, 199-200.

community from which it derives flavour, character and efficacy.[23]

So the place of community, and covenanted relationship with God and others, is crucial in our human 'becomingness'. It is the *communion* of differing stories, the stories of God, the stories of other people, that we find our voice and our own unique story. A large proportion of people in emerging Churches have come from pretty extreme fundamentalist expressions of faith. Many are therefore very cynical about prayer and the Bible, largely because they have experienced abuses of both. It is therefore crucial for emerging churches to provide the opportunity for deeper expressions of prayer, and a re-engagement with the bible, which for some, is really difficult.

It is important here to grasp the role of Church as an 'interpretative community'.[24] Within the intimacy of relationship, various truths, and interpretations can be discussed and owned by the community. Although the Bible was inspired by God it, was written by human beings and is therefore not without error. Comprehension of the bible requires the use of human sense organs and the mind. Whilst this may at times be a God inspired activity, it is also very human. The power of interpretative communities is their ability to balance reason with experience and understanding, so that the Holy Spirit can promote a shared understanding. Being utterly counter-fundamentalist, this approach enables people to hold onto their own thoughts and understanding. It enables ongoing dialogue, and the sense that knowledge continually unfolds through transcendent encounter. New thinking that emerges as communities explore their tradition can be tested against the established. Shared language and worldview are constructed socially, as a subjective, shared attempt to express meaning about God and existence. This shared narrative then becomes the narrative of the individual. Openness to new meaning is very healthy if it remains in the context of the ongoing tradition. This is not so easy in groups that do not have a deep understanding of tradition, and the danger of 'throwing the baby out with the bathwater' becomes acute. Many emerging churches have weekly groups that operate as interpretative forums, encourage learning through discussion and experience – also yet another form of transcendent encounter. Group

---

[23] Ibid, 200.
[24] Attributed to Stanley Hauerwas in P. Janowiak, *The Holy Preaching: The Sacramentality of the Word in the Liturgical Assembly*, (Collegeville, USA: Liturgical Press, 2000), 151.

consensus acts as a healthy 'reality check' of the truth of what is being said.

Being this type of Church is far from easy. There is real danger that powerful, charismatic characters will manipulate meaning, and subvert the community. Real, transparent and agreed governance structures are important to prevent such abuses. Such forms of church do not work if numbers rise to the point where meetings become impersonal. I don't think you can do this form of church in numbers greater than one hundred and twenty, and around half this number is preferable. If an interpretative community is going to draw effectively on contemplative spirituality, there needs to be a high regard to openness, discernment and action. Openness should be characterised by active and respectful listening to the views of others, and by a sense of humility when before the unfamiliar, the new and the unexpected.[25] This form of discernment, says McCarthy:

> *invites us to put our lives in dialogue with the tradition through prayer, reflection, meditation, individual and group guidance, and other practices. They encourage attentive listening and awareness of how we are being called and where we are being led...looking for certain signs such as a sense of inner and outer freedom, an awareness of the connectedness and interrelation of all creation, a rootedness in tradition coupled with openness to the new, and a sense of deep inner peace.*[26]

> *[Such discernment] can help us to retrieve the role of community in nurturing a deep spiritual life. It can provide the means for examining and critiquing both ancient and contemporary forms of community living and it can assist us in reconstructing forms of community life which are real and effective in today's society.*[27]

Whilst these forms of spiritual community are very hard to live, the rewards are great when we get it right. There are tools that can assist us in this pursuit. Firstly, as we discussed previously there is real power in the formulation of a rhythm of life to help develop the interpretative dimension of the community. The pattern of spirituality discussed in this chapter resonates with the foundational vision of many

---

[25] *Ibid*, 200-1.
[26] *Ibid*, 201.
[27] *Ibid*, 204.

monastic and new monastic movements. The Moot Community's Rhythm of Life has helped us develop our own sense of the narrative of the Christian tradition of which we are a part. The practice of hospitality is vital, particularly for engaging with people who have had no church experience. From my own experience, unconditional hospitality has been the key to enabling this way of being church to happen. I am still fostering friendships with spiritual tourists who have surfed the edges of Moot since its inception. However, the rewards of hospitality cannot be reaped overnight, it takes years worth of commitment. My friend Michael Volland literally walked around Gloucester for several months talking to people in all sorts of places, miles away from the church, with a view to building an incarnational expression of church. A transcendent model of contextual theology enables us to trust God to be present as we are attentive to the conversations and meetings we have in the ordinariness of life.

After all, this is the form of church that helped form me into the person and Christian I am today. The self-confidence I gained helped me believe I could be an Occupational Therapist and eventually, staggeringly, an Anglican Priest. These forms of church have been crucial in my own walk through life.

However, human becoming through community is not just about contemplation, participation and worship. There are also very real opportunities for practical action. This is connected with the very real need for churches to consider commitment to place as well as network. Some examples of practical action are those who work with the homeless, who set up cafés to connect with local people in public space, those who are involved in social care. After all, the source of our inspiration, the Monks and Friars of the pre-modern period, were very involved in practical projects with the poor and needy. I suggest that all Christian communities need to consider how they can practically serve their local communities – both of place and network - with a commitment to being present to ordinary people through loving service. Personally I love the idea that the Church's café becomes the hub of the local community. A number of emerging Churches have done precisely this, and their communities have become profound places of inclusion, love, and service. A community taking on such a project, with a degree of maturity in contemplative prayer, can really enable growth through giving rather than taking and consumption.

In a world of so much need, there is only so much our communities can sustain before they fall into the trap of attempting, and inevitably failing, to fulfil the roll of social services. Nevertheless, there are real opportunities for engagement and an open-ness to doing so is the place to start. We need to remember that when our communities reflect the love and acceptance of the Triune God they can truly become places of transformation and growth. No one expresses this better than Jean Vanier, whose whole life was centred on developing community as a profound expression of becoming and healing. He supported adults with learning difficulties whose experience of rejection and loss of identity had been internalised in quite extreme ways. In his community these individuals became connected and experienced belonging, love and forgiveness. This led to transformation (human becoming) as they followed the example modelled by in Christ, and the Trinity more generally.

This sounds good in theory, but how does one practically do this type of Christian Community? For Jean Vanier, it begins with following the Trinitarian God of creative love:

> *To the poverty of our human minds the possibility of a destiny conceived by God, and freedom, seem contradictory. Yet it is not so. For the wisdom of God and God's respect for each person is so great, that a destiny of ultimate fulfilment, and individual freedom, are gently married, and the glory of God and of creation flows from this union. God has the secret of loving us to freedom, inviting us to share in the creativity of love. Because so many of us have experienced a love coming from parents – or others – that is stifling or crippling or possessive, it is difficult to believe we are loved by a love that brings us to freedom, and that God's plan goes far beyond the wonder and beauty of the creation we know ... Yes the deepest song of everything in creation reflects the unity of the Trinity: three persons poured out in love for one another.*[28]

The starting place of community is the willingness work at the task, to believe that a group of acquaintances can become community. As we follow Christ,[29] the community eventually becomes more inter-related, and so reflects God's perichoretic nature. Christ expressed the becoming of God in how he lived and related to others, starting with the disciples. As the title of this book would suggest, the 'becoming of God' is the basic premise with I most desire to challenge the Church.

---

[28] J Vanier, *The Broken Body,* (London: DLT, 1988), 26-28.
[29] Vanier, *The Broken,* 26-62.

We must aim to reflect this becoming in our communities as we follow the example modelled by the trinitarian God.

The Becoming of Community

One of the greatest myths today, is that personal fulfilment is to do with pleasure or happiness, and a rejection of the idea that pain has anything to do with authentic living.

> *So many of us flee from people crying out in pain, people who are broken. We hide in a world of distraction and pleasure or in 'things to do'...Or if we do not flee from suffering perhaps we revolt in anger...Many people who appear powerful and successful can also feel worthless deep inside themselves. They have money, power, education, status, but they lack what is essential: a heart that is free and loving, the knowledge that they are loved. They seem unable to relate, and feel broken and empty inside...They too feel they belong to no one. They feel that terrible pain of being unable to love, of isolation, unable to break out of their shell to relate with trust and faithfulness, in communion with others.*[30]

A starting place for Christian community is the dispelling of the myth that pain and suffering have nothing to do with the human journey of becoming. Generally speaking, pain and suffering is made worse by isolation and exclusion. There is nothing more powerful than sharing ones pain in community, and finding support and care. Somehow, knowing that we are cared for, and that our carers suffer similarly, makes our pain all the more bearable. Further, being connected with others who are also in pain helps us develop adaptive coping strategies. This is fairly obvious stuff; after all it is the basis of the hugely successful '12 step programme'. Such groups meet regularly for mutual support and to develop coping strategies, with appeal to a higher power. Both Vanier and the followers of '12 step' have discovered the power of spiritual community. A community that is steeped in the Christian narrative, and that draws inspiration from the perichoretic relationships of the Trinity, can be hugely transformative.

> *In the beauty and fragility of this experience [of community] lies also its pain. In awakening our capacity to love, it awakens*

---

[30] Vanier, *The Broken*, 1, 13.

> *what is deepest in us which includes our vulnerability and sensitivity...Community provides the necessary safeguards and limits but also the support to allow us to live fully these experiences of joy and pain. Community gives the confirmation we need to remain faithful. It can provide also the challenge we need to go forward, so that we can live these experiences as times of growth on our pilgrimage, which is both a journey to greater wisdom and to the deeper rooting of our being.[31]*

However, maintaining a healthy community, when many of its members are in pain, must be carefully managed, so as to promote healthy inter-dependency and not co-dependency. This is why '12 step' groups must have skilled facilitators. In the context of community, this can be self-regulating, where regular discussions are governed by agreed 'ground rules' aimed at building trust and openness. An effective community must be grounded in a commitment to openness and the sharing of love and support in the midst of deep pain.

The Becoming of Belonging
The achievement of openness and honesty are important milestones in the growth of any community. However, many flounder in the attempt to establish the vital sense of trust and belonging:

> *The Christian churches seem to many people irrelevant, for they too are more a cause of division and of war than a source of unity and peace.[32]*

Churches need to rediscover how to become inclusive communities that inspire people to go deeper with the trinitarian God. Communities that encourage trust and belonging can become transformative communities:

> *The sense of belonging flows from trust: trust is the gradual acceptance of others as they are with their gifts and their limits, each one with the call of Jesus. And this leads to the realization that the body of community is not perfectly whole and cannot be, that this is our human condition. And it is all right for us to be less than perfect. We must not weep over our*

---

[31] Vanier, *The Broken*, 94-6.
[32] Vanier, *The Broken*, 15.

> *imperfections. We are not judged for being defective. Our God knows that in so many ways we are lame and half-blind...but we can walk together in hope, celebrating that we are loved in our brokenness.*[33]

A truly open community is one where those who do not believe can participate and belong, alongside those who do. This can be a challenge, but it is very much within our grasp. Many emerging Churches are committed to this, knowing that people often need to work out who they are in a safe place, before they realise their need for God. The temptation in this context is to dumb down on the Christian centeredness of the group, but quite the opposite is required if people are to have a positive experience of Christian community. Building such communities is really tough, and takes a long time, but the rewards once established are substantial.

The Becoming of Forgiveness
Community at base is the sense of 'common unity' or 'at-one-ment'. If unity is to be maintained, there must be a commitment to forgiveness. This is particularly difficult in communities that are characterised by a diversity of behaviour and values, as emerging Churches often are. Additionally, our wider culture is not good at forgiveness. When public figures are disgraced, there is very little sense of redemption. No community centred on love, trust and belonging can be maintained without a commitment to forgiveness. Now this is not a green light for aggressive or dehumanising behaviour, but rather an acceptance that we are incomplete and will make mistakes. A healthy discipline worth considering for individuals committed to Christian community is external spiritual direction or mentoring. Awareness of self (strengths and weaknesses) is vital in negotiating a healthy spiritual community. Otherwise, our emotional brokenness will always be projected into the community. Forgiveness is the choice to let go, to rise above, and to choose approaches centred on meditation and finding the common good. Where this is modelled it can lead to profound community:

> *Forgiveness is the source and the rock of those who share their lives: to forgive each day, to forgive and forgive and forgive, and to be forgiven just as many times...Forgiveness is the cement that bonds us together: it is the source of unity; it is the*

---
[33] *Ibid*, 98-9.

> *quality of love; that draws togetherness out of separation... Forgiveness is letting go of unrealistic expectations of others and of the desire that they be other than they are. Forgiveness is liberating others to be themselves, not making them feel guilty for what may have been...Forgiveness is to follow Jesus, to be like him, for he came to give and forgive, to take from the shoulders of people the yoke of guilt that locks them into a prison of sadness and sterility, and prevents them from flowing and living freely.*[34]

Forgiveness is so profoundly counter-cultural and uncommon, that it must be learnt. Therefore it must firstly be modelled in community. One cannot assume that the ability to forgive follows directly from the intellectual comprehension of it. Feelings go deep, and rising above our own pain and insecurity is one of the greatest challenges facing us as human becomings. Often, communities that have initially established trust, belonging and love, fail because of division created by a lack of forgiveness.

The Becoming of Hope

When a community practises love, openness to joy and pain, belonging and forgiveness, it becomes a profoundly hopeful place – an unfortunately rare phenomenon in our world today:

> *Helping each other, growing in trust, living in thanksgiving, learning to forgive, opening up to others, welcoming them, and striving to bring peace and hope to our world. So it is that we come to put down roots in community – not because it is perfect and wonderful, but because we believe that Jesus called us together. It is where we belong and are called to grow and to serve.*[35]

A community that is able to live this way, no matter how imperfectly has a lot to give to the world. When coupled with a healthy, culturally relevant expression of worship, mission and community, it can be a potent expression of deep Christian faith. Unfortunately such hope-driven Christian communities are rare, a factor that I believe relates directly to state of decline the Church now finds itself in.

---

[34] *Ibid*, 106-7.
[35] *Ibid*, 99.

The Becoming of Justice

Once people find hope, forgiveness, openness, belonging and community, it is hoped that they will have had personal experience of the love of God. This may take a long time, but often, as story God's story and the community's story become the individuals' story there is a shift from consumption to production, from taking to giving. Some experience God through loving acts of service, others through spiritual encounters. Regardless of which medium it is, the justice and inclusion experienced in the perichoretic community inevitably becomes the model to follow. In this way, our communities become characterised justice, peace, and ministry to the poor, excluded or oppressed. We can then be thought of as being in culture but not of it. The emerging Church is one of a number of recent innovations in the Christian Church that has social, economic and ecological justice as foundational values. Justice and mercy are deeply humanising forces in our world, where thinking globally and acting locally can have significant impact. This is not an easy journey – Christ, many Saints of the Church, and plenty of modern day figures such as Martin Luther King Junior were killed for similar values. As Eberhard Arnold said:

> *We must live in community because we take our stand in the spiritual fight on the side of all those who fight for freedom, unity, peace, and social justice...Yet we are not the driving force in this – it is we who have been driven and who must be urged on.*[36]

If Church communities desire to become places of love, belonging, forgiveness, hope and justice, they will follow the values of the perichoretic Godhead. The missional and evangelistic impact of Church modelled on the very becoming of G-d could be enormous.

Reflection

Two years ago I was taken to Margate, Kent, to experience an interesting Anglican church that was a cross between a charismatic evangelical and a fresh expression of church. I had been really cynical and did not want to go. However, I was shocked by the challenge I encountered. The Church was situated in a deprived area of Margate that had become a ghetto for drug addicts, child offenders and asylum

---

[36] E Arnold, *We Live in Community,* (Robertsbridge, East Sussex: Plough Publishing House, 1995), 5, 30.

seekers. Stories from a recent baptism service conducted by those living in local temporary accommodation were profoundly moving. God had met with them in profound ways in the midst of their pain, giving many the impetus needed to sort their lives out. Whole families, separated through legal proceedings, crime and other factors, came together and celebrated in the joy of the moment, before they were separated and went to various custodial places. The depth of relationship spoke of a very real sense of loving commitment in that community. In the brief moments of the worship service, the Church had enabled those present to experience a transcendent encounter with God. It is hoped that these very real encounters, would encourage many to seek God's help in facing the darker side of their lives. I was truly humbled by the experience. Thinking about it afterward, I realised that this is the power of a church that chooses to reflect the Triune God in what it does and says. The next challenge for that church is how it can maintain such a ministry and participative community. We also face the same challenge: are we prepared to live this costly way in our postmodern world?

Chapter Eight

Where from here?
A vision of unity in diversity

It was Immanuel Kant (1724-1804) who said *'the doctrine of the Trinity provides nothing, absolutely nothing, of practical value, even if one claims to understand it; still less when one is convinced that it far surpasses our understanding... [it] offers absolutely no guidance for conduct.*[1]

Clearly everything I have argued in this book so far is in opposition to Kant's judgement of the trinity. I believe that an understanding of the Trinity as unity in diversity can profoundly help the church to learn a more nurturing and loving way to live together in difference. However, before we consider this, we need to face the issue of leadership in the church.

You may have noticed that I haven't mentioned anything about church leadership up until this point. I wanted to fully explore community first, and in my experience, as soon as community is mentioned, ordination and leadership tend to dominate the discussion.

---

[1] C A Hall, *Learning Theology with the Church Fathers,* (Leicester: IVP), in B Edgar, *The Message of the Trinity,* (Leicester, 2004), 22, 53.

However, I do think trinitarian ecclesiology presents a distinct challenge to current understandings of leadership. Therefore we must to return to Augustine, the *Filioque* clause and the Doctrine of the Trinity.

Unfortunately, the consequence of Augustine's inclusion of the *filioque* clause in the Nicene Creed, was to create an internal hierarchy within the nature of God. There is no evidence in scripture at all about this internal hierarchy, and it is at odds with the Cappadocian Fathers understanding of the Trinity. Nevertheless, it was to prove very useful when having to justify the power and office of the Bishops, and the Pope in Rome. What was modelled by God, should be imitated by the Church, or so it was argued. With this view of the Trinity, Priests and Bishops were not just important elements of administration, but the centre and life of the church. For Volf, the episcopocentric model of the Church (endorsed by Ratzinger, the current Pope) is not consistent with a the non-*filioque* version of the Nicene Creed:[2]

> *Over the course of this investigation, I have tried to show (1) that the church is not a single subject, but rather a communion of interdependent subjects, (2) that the mediation of salvation occurs not only through office-holders, but also through all other members of the church, and (3) that the church is constituted by the Holy Spirit not so much by way of the institution of office as through a communal confession in which Christians speak the word of God to one another. From these three basic theological convictions, it follows that the life and structure of church cannot be episcopocentric. The church is not a monocentric-bipolar community, however articulated, but rather fundamentally, a polycentric community.*[3]

For Volf, the Laity are of equal importance as those in office, because the gifts of the Holy Spirit are universal, and employed by the whole church in service to the world:

> *Universal distribution of the charismata implies common responsibility for the life of the church. Such common responsibility is compatible with the particular charismata of leadership. In the context of universal distribution of charismata, however, such leadership acquires a new profile. It*

---

[2] Volf, *After*, 221-234.
[3] *Ibid*, 224.

> *cannot be the task of leaders, ordained or not, to do everything in the church themselves. This would lead to hypertrophy of this one member of the body of Christ and to the fateful atrophy of all other members. The task of leaders is first to animate all the members of the church to engage their pluriform charismatic activities, and then to coordinate these activities.*[4]

Here leadership is modelled in servant form, and is akin to coordination, much like the role of a conductor of an orchestra or a curator of an art gallery. The issue then is giving people room to exercise their ministry accountably within the community. Much of this learning has been appropriated by the emerging Church, with emphasis is given to shared leadership and leadership by event. The model is centred on the participation of the whole church as an event, a deeply trinitarian idea. Polycentric communities are characterised by equality, which is distorted by the implications of the *filioque* clause. This means that Ordination, and the offices of Priest and Bishop are reframed by the context of servant ministry. Offices of charismata and empowered by the Holy Spirit they may be, but they are roles of function, not of power and hierarchy.

Unsurprisingly this is not such a problem in the East, where priests were seen as servants of the church, and otherwise normal people who could marry and have families. Bishops were seen as the wise grandees of the church, respected and listened to, but without the power invested in Western Bishops. It is clear that if the western historic churches continue in this period of post-Christendom and disestablishmentarianism, to endorse a hierarchical, episcopocentric model of Church, that the laity will only be further disempowered and alienated. As we have already discussed, some emerging churches have sought permission from their Diocesan Bishop to set up new monastic chapters. Oxford groups mayBE and hOME have Chapters with an Abbot and Prior, where the Prior is appointed by community election. Again these offices are modelled on service not on power. Leadership needs to be reframed as servanthood, with the function of empowering and nurturing the laity. This clearly models a trinitarian way of being church, being centred on unity in diversity.

If the global Church is to develop unity in diversity, an appreciation of trinitarian ecclesiology is vital. This involves an approach modelled in the love of God, and seeking the full expression

---

[4] *Ibid*, 230.

of humanity in all our difference. The core creedal statement of the Church as one, holy, catholic and apostolic, seems most applicable. This would mean that the world church is fully present only when thinking about itself as catholic and protestant, conservative and liberal. Only together can the church be fully Church. If it could catch up with God's vision of its nature, the way it relates to the world, and itself, would be vastly improved. I have deep admiration for Rowan Williams, the current Archbishop of Canterbury, for his extremely deep understanding, and subtle appreciation of this. If he led in an episcopocentric way, he would attempt to use power politics to bring unity in conformity. He does not do this. Instead he is often publicly silent, whilst working hard behind the scenes to help opposing forces meet and talk to each other. To some he has appeared weak, but for me, he is seeking to serve the church out of a vision of unity in diversity. He draws on Reformation-period Anglican history, when violent battles raged between rival claims to unity in conformity. No in this post-Christendom world, the vision of unity in diversity gives great insight into how the church could move forward in a more relational way.

As an alternative to fundamentalism, it enables an approach that has a high regard towards God and Scripture as well as to culture and being human. Some of this is being modelled in emerging and fresh expressions of church, but there is still more need for a deep, authentic Christian spirituality for our postmodern age. As Volf says:

> *A participative model of church requires more than just values and practices that correspond to participative institutions. The church is not first of all a realm of moral purposes; it is the anticipation, constituted by the presence of the Spirit of God, of the eschatological gathering of the entire people of God in communion with the triune God. Hence the church needs the vivifying presence of the Spirit, and without this presence, even a church with a decentralised participative structure and culture will become sterile, and perhaps more sterile even than a hierarchical church. For it will either have to operate with more subtle or open forms of coercion. Successful participative church life must be sustained by deep spirituality. Only the person who lives from the Spirit of communion (2 Cor. 13:13) can participate authentically in the life of the ecclesial community.*[5]

---

[5] Volf, *After*, 257.

The hunger for this deep spirituality, that must become the focus for the future, is the inevitable consequence of our techno-consumer society. The great rise in spiritual tourism presents to the Church, the challenge of whether it is willing to recognise the reality of this new context. Unfortunately there is an enormous amount of fear in the churches, which have a tendency to look back rather than forwards. The increasingly fractured relations between evangelical and catholic, and conservative and liberal, in all denominations, exacerbates this even more. Graham Cray put this well recently:

> *Postmodern people are more likely to come to faith through experience which leads to understanding of doctrine than through prior intellectual assent. But one of the tragedies of today is that some elements of the Church are now so firmly secularised in their disbelief in the supernatural that they have nothing to say to a culture which increasingly takes spirituality and the supernatural for granted.*[6]

It appears to me that the Church in the West must engage with the task of exploring an authentic Christian spirituality that is able to connect with our current postmodern expression of new mysticism. The Deep Church and emerging Church, though small movements, are significant responses to this challenge. However, with the greatest of respect, both are still minority sports in the UK church. Although Fresh Expressions has given permission for mission-centered experimental forms of churches, it again has not birthed very many radical groups engaging with this brave new world. Additionally, many of those already in existence could be accused of being the same product, but with a little window dressing.

One project that does model this unity in diversity model, and a profound vision of engaging with new mysticism, is St Andrews Church, Holborn. Here a visionary vicar has drawn a group of Charismatic evangelicals, an orthodox icon making community, some Monks from Rome, together with some catholic Anglicans. All are very excited by this co-operation, sharing a strong sense of the participation of the Holy Spirit in their endeavor to put the *Friar* back into the Blackfriars area of London. Already the church has become a place of visitation and pilgrimage. Underneath the Church building is a natural well, which has become the venue of a new healing centre. There is a

---

[6] G Cray quoted in Y Richmond et al., *Evangelism*, 14.

shared understanding of perichoresis, kenosis and panentheism. If they get this mix right, it could be a great example of new, missional ecumenism engaging with new mysticism.

My hope for the emerging Church is for the growth of new monasticism. I am excited by the thought of small contextual Friaries, offering radical hospitality and access to a reframed Christian contemplative tradition, growing up all around the country. However, the movement needs a contemporary incarnation of Evelyn Underhill (a Christian Mystic of the early twentieth century) to bring this spirituality to life in the 21st century. Many of the new monastic groups are attempting to set up intentional, residential communities, with radical hospitality through café church, arts, alternative worship and contemplative patterns of prayer and meditation. Though are few in number, some have taken root in various locations in the UK. It is my own personal hope that the potent combination of innovative hospitality and a spiritual patterning of life will allow people to directly experience God.

A great example of this is the story of Ian Cron, who had a stress related breakdown. Following the death of a young girl, he began to seek God for wholeness and acceptance. In his quest he followed St Francis, learning from the original Christian monks about life, and its climax, the experience of God through the Eucharist:

> *Kenny had a sense of the poetic. He took us to a six o'clock Mass in one of the side chapels at Saint John Lateran. It was only fitting that our last stop would be at the site where the Franciscan Order had received a blessing from the pope to minister to the world...when we knelt at the altar to receive Communion, all of my confidence quickly withered. When the elderly priest came to me, I held out my cupped hands to receive the communion host. The old priest, however suffered from a slight tremor in his hands, so I had to keep moving my own to try and position them under his to receive the round wafer...Just when it looked like the exchange might end happily,...the wafer fell between the cracks of my coupled hands and hit the stone floor of the altar in front of me...I froze. I had fumbled Jesus. God bless that palsied old priest. Without so much as skipping a beat, he reverently picked up the host, held it to heaven, and murmured, "Veni, veni, Sancte Spiritu", then closed his eyes and received it himself. He took another wafer from the communion paten and waveringly placed it*

> *securely in the nest formed by my outstretched hands. Gazing deeply into my eyes, he said "My son, this is the body of Christ". What happened next is difficult to explain and perhaps, as with all mysteries, it is unwise to try. All I know is that in the moment of reception I was visited by God. Perhaps it was the goodness of the priest and his graciousness that silently opened a portal through which I momentarily made contact with the divine life. Or maybe it was the Eucharist itself – the host mingling with my brokenness, dissolving in saliva, coming to rest in the shallows of my heart's confusion. Kneeling at the altar, I was overwhelmed by the sense that my fragmented and discontinuous life actually made sense.*[7].

This profound sense of transcendent encounter with God is what the Church must strive to model. I believe it can come through manifold traditions - contemplative prayer, silence, charismatic worship - you name it, God can use it. The key thing is confidence in the church and in God that such things are possible. A change in skill sets for leaders of the church will be required. The practice of contemplative prayer has been seen as optional for church leaders. I would argue that in the context of a culture of new mysticism, it is essential. All trained leaders need to have good group listening and facilitation skills, the ability to enable and inspire, all these are essential. Leaders ought also to be familiar with the ancient tradition of the church, considering themselves custodians of it, so as to enable postmodern pilgrims to learn of its richness. In other words, this means being able to support a focus on Ancient:Future practice, reframing resources of the past into the contemporary context. Many have done just this with labyrinth prayer walks, contemplative prayer, chanting, and Stations of the Cross. There are many ancient mediums which effectively enable encounter the Triune God. It is all down to the imagination and creativity of church.

The greatest challenge remains, how do we be Church in a consumptive, technological, business oriented world, but not of it. I am concerned about the lack of knowledge of the faith many Christians seem to suffer from. There is a tribal attitude, now very entrenched, where ones Christian identity is defined by how we are 'not like them'. I am also concerned that many churches operate on essentially the same

---

[7] Ian Morgan Cron, *Chasing Francis,* (Colorado Springs: Navpress, 2006), 177-8.

terms as corporate business. It hit me quite recently, that such forms of church tend to downplay the values of Trinitarian ecclesiology and an understanding of unity in diversity.

The models explored in Avery Dulles' insightful book, *Models of Church,* are a reflection of the varied emphases placed on the person of Christ. Briefly, the models, and their ecclesiastical corollaries, are as follows: God as King - Church as political society, God as Trinity - Church as mystical communion, God as Sacramental - Church as Sacrament, God as Servant - Church as servant, God as Proclaimer - Church as Herald, and finally, God as teacher - Church as discipler. These are pretty well known, and I have already covered the Church as mystical communion, and sacrament models in this book. I would like to add another model, the increasing presence of which deeply troubles me, mainly because I don't believe its consequences have been thought through. It is the 'Church as business' model. It seems to have seeped in with little questioning due to the financial pressures of the modern world. As far I am aware however, there is as yet very little written about it, even though very many churches have absorbed it. Clearly this model is not based on the significance of Christ, but purely on business sense.

I am concerned that it does not foster a high view of Church as an alternative, inclusive community. Instead the emphasis is on something of a process model. In my experience, the PCC of a church like this quickly becomes the Board, your congregants become share holders, and the church becomes divided into various departments sustaining different business activities. Where is the place of the poor in this model? Can those of little economic or work value find a place here? And what of those without business skills? For me this is of much greater concern to the Church at large than the hot-potato issues, such as sexuality and gender, which these Churches often champion. So why is the church so silent on this issue?

In some ways I can trace the development of alternative worship and the emerging Church as a reaction to churches that were increasingly dehumanising in their business approach – they had made the shift from fluid community to organisation. I would argue that many of the "successful" churches in London are built on a model of 'Church as Business', and that they visibly demonstrate its weakness. The question needs to be asked how, if they are to be contextual and authentic, are these churches being in but not of business culture? I think many of us who have been part of such churches have a sorry tale to tell. Vicars seem to operate as powerful managing directors with significant financial and political power. The danger of distortion to the function of the 'body of Christ' is substantial.

Don't get me wrong, I am not against business innovation or the need for creative entrepreneurialism where it is considered and used wisely. However, I am concerned that many do not seem to be aware of the consequences of taking on capitalist and business models of the church. For me, the greatest downside is that the mission activities of such churches cannot be counter to business values. They target the powerful, rich and successful, avoiding the poor the disadvantaged, and have a very Christendom focused approach to Church and mission.

The mystical communion model, coupled with the sacramental model, is the form of church required to counter the syncretism of 'church as business'. Our challenge in the 21st century is to reengage with the poor who are increasingly excluded from a society defined by consumerism and technology. If anything, predictions appear to suggest that society will further fragment between the 'haves' and the 'have nots'. Where will the church be? Will it seek to engage with the bored youth on our streets with nothing to do and nowhere to go? It seems that extremism and hate have found a breeding ground amongst the poor, so it is vital that the Church gets its hands dirty by engaging with both socio-economic extremes. After all, is this not where Christ by the Holy Spirit will draw us?

All this aside, I am optimistic that a contemporary form of deep spirituality, that can draw together the historic traditions, and bring the heart of the faith to our contemporary culture, is now taking shape. Via a model of unity in diversity, renewed transcendence, and the mystical transformation of encounter with the Trinity, it will bring hope and real encounter back to our world.

> *The Trinity is the source of mission because the sending of the church into the world is a continuation of the Father's love which led to a sending of the Son and Spirit, Trinitarian love (not fear, obligation or duty) is what lies at the heart of Christian mission (Matthew 28:19).*[8]

So how do we maintain this deep spirituality in the West? How do we sustain a stronger trinitarian theology and ecclesiology that avoids the traditional binary and hierarchical manifestation?

---

[8] Edgar, *The Message of the Trinity*, 29.

I return to Pete Rollins, the Emerging Church and the language of Icons:

> *Those within the emerging conversation find unity not by a type of cloning which all Christians are encouraged to believe the same thing...speaking of God is but only ever speaking about our understanding of God...this approach diligently maintains a conceptual distance between ourselves and God, one which approaches the divine mystery as something to be transformed by rather than solved by...*[9]

> *To treat something as an icon is to view particular words, images or experiences as aids in contemplation of that which cannot be reduced to words, images or experience. Not only this, but the icon represents a place where God touches humanity. Consequently, icons are only the place where we contemplate God, they also act as the place that God uses in order to communicate with us...In this iconic understanding, our thoughts concerning God are directed towards God in love rather than enslaving God with words.*[10]

There is great wisdom in these words. We must pursue a form of faith that holds in tension knowing and unknowing, with an emphasis on knowing God through contemplative forms of prayer and worship. Maybe having an awareness of the potential idolatry of words frees both God and us. I am convinced that the combination of this iconic understanding of the triune God and the disciplines of contemplative prayer and worship, will help the Christian faith to rediscover its full place in society. To do this, the church must develop a language and practices that relate to our consumptive and technological culture. However, there must be a commitment to transcend the weaknesses of Western theological thinking, some of which I have outlined here.

So we finish where we started – remembering the insights of the emerging Church conversation – that we must not misuse our understandings of the Trinity to project fixed understandings of God. Trinitarians is an imperfect understanding drawing on the spiritual experiences of people with the One God in three persons. It is however,

---

[9] Rollins, *How*, 32.
[10] Rollins, *How*, 38, 40.

in my opinion, the best construct amongst other imperfect constructs. A distinctive understanding.

Instead we must remember that theology is the place where God speaks into human discourse, and that as we do mission, it points people to the divine. Religious truth is that which transforms reality rather than that which describes it. In worship and mission we seek to contemplate God, who in turn touches and communicates with humanity. If Church is truly modelled on this approach, it will meet deeply with contemporary culture. And maybe for first real time, Churches of all different traditions can model unity in diversity.

Instead of more theory, the next chapter is reserved for prayer, contemplation and worship. I encourage you to seek God as you consider the issues covered in this book. Thanks for journeying with me.

Ian Mobsby
January 2008.

The Author
Ian Mobsby is an Ordained Anglican Priest who has eighteen years experience researching and working with Emerging and Fresh Expressions of Church. He is a founder member for two projects including the Moot Community in Central London. In addition, Ian is an Associate Missioner of the Archbishop's Fresh Expressions Team in England, and an Associate Lecturer for two Colleges that training Ordained Pioneer Ministers. Ian has lectured extensively in the UK, USA and New Zealand.

Chapter Nine

Trinitarian Devotions

This chapter includes a number of poems and devotionals to promote exploration through imaginative encounter.

Perichoresis - The Divine Dance of God
by Ian Mobsby

Heads bowing, hands sharing, hearts racing
Feet poised suspended in the support of the other.
Holy Three yet one, laugh, cry, celebrate and lament their co-creativity.

Time burst out as the by-product of a hurling helix
of mystical presence
swaying through the dance.
Life and all things became real
Out of the dynamic of joy and love expressed in movement.

The Creator led the dance from beginning to incarnation,
The Redeemer led the dance from incarnation to Pentecost
The Companion leads the dance now from the time of the church
to the consummation.
But Holy dance,
don't slow down,
don't wait on us inattentive humanity.

Free us Holy Three in one to learn the dance
Teach us to be free from our selfishness and greed
Let us relearn how to dance spiritually
And be a blessing to the Cosmos
And be the spiritual community
The dancing God calls us to be

Amen

Periochoresis by Pádraig Twomey

perfectly held in one another's being

every breathing in is echoed

richly in another breathing out.

in all this movement of the
one into the other, a

circle with no start and with no ending, we are

harboured in the sight, scooped up in the wildlight

of the three loves flowing here as one,

resonant with understanding, all our red

earth's grief is managing to find a voice, and find a

story, swept up in this all-enfolding presence

individual, indivisible, in the never ending present vision

of the

simple, see the three who are

Perichoresis
by Mike Radcliffe

On Friday nights we went to clubs
until we noticed something that
night when the three of them came and took
over the regular dancing. So

Did the Creator throw shapes on the
dance floor whilst dancing a salsa that
turned all the heads of the punters there?

Vogueing away while the other two
scattered. They took up their places but
somehow remaining together there

How the Companion perfected that
fight in a way that was calming them.
Making them friends from thereon until

Now. The Revealer is reveling
showing us all just a little too
much how its done by his lead for us

Dancing together while beckoning onlookers
come on and join us, and have a good
time. Doesn't matter it's happening.

Keeping the rhythm up copying
maybe looked easy as no-one would
dare to reject their advances then

in pairs we couldn't make it work
and groups of us tried sussing out
as individuals put together
were fitting triplets into four time.

We stopped the dancing, getting going
on paper noting down what happened
as dancing disappeared while writing
and scrapping round some bits of paper.

Moot Ikon – The Trinity
By Michael L Radcliffe

Isaac Laughed
by Bowie Snodgrass

First Sarah laughed –
When three angels said
She would bear a son.
Even in my old age?!

Then Isaac laughed,
Going along with his dad,
Sure, we'll do the sacrifice,
I will journey with you.

So Abraham took him,
Set him on an altar –
When an angel appeared
From God and laughed.

Take Your Place
By Tara Lamont Eastman

This hunger that draws me closer to You.
This thirst that brings me back to Truth.
Where can these needs elsewhere be met?
Sifting through the shallow,
This pushes past the rest.

The Bread, the Wine -
made real in time.
The Body, the Blood -
fills my needs in love.

Cups to fill,
Bread to break -
Each day holds a Eucharist...
Take your place.

Brought together in one place,
We all are drawn by Your grace.
All as one and each one seen -
How does this table draws us?
So unpredictable and unclean.

The Bread, the Wine -
made real in time.
The Body, the Blood -
fills my needs in love.

Cups to fill,
Bread to break -
Each day holds a Eucharist...
Take your place.

Carry this meal to the heart of the world.
Carry the message of hope restored.
Sit and share this meal and rest -
Forgiveness offered, conversation blessed.

The Bread, the Wine -
made real in time.
The Body, the Blood -
fills my needs in love.

Cups to fill,
Bread to break -
Each day holds a Eucharist...
Take your place.

Cups to fill,
Bread to break -
Each day holds a Eucharist...
Take your place.